This dissertation was conducted under the direction of Sister Mary Verone Wohlwend, S.N.D., and read by the Right Reverend Monsignor Francis J. Houlahan, and Sister Mary Rita Buddeke, S.N.D. deN.

TEACHING ENGLISH AS A FOREIGN LANGUAGE
TO CHILDREN: FIRST THREE GRADES

by

Eva R. Borrego

A Dissertation

THE CATHOLIC UNIVERSITY OF AMERICA

1968

Printed in 1974 by

R AND E RESEARCH ASSOCIATES
4843 Mission Street, San Francisco 94112
18581 McFarland Avenue, Saratoga, California 95070

Publishers and Distributors of Ethnic Studies
Editor: Adam S. Eterovich
Publisher: Robert D. Reed

Library of Congress Card Catalog Number

74-76758

ISBN

0-88247-282-8

ACKNOWLEDGMENTS

The author wishes to express her grateful appreciation for the valuable assistance rendered by the many persons cooperating in this report. She is particularly indebted to Rt. Rev. Msgr. Houlahan, Sister Verone Wohlwend, and Sister Rita Buddeke whose constant guidance and generous help convoyed the entire work to its completion.

To Elvira Espinosa, Achsa Spahr, Alice Wright, William C. Meyer, and Dale Lorimer the author is deeply indebted for helpful support and understanding so willingly given. Finally, the writer wishes to thank Mrs. Vada Showalter for her generous efforts in typing this report.

TABLE OF CONTENTS

LIST OF TABLES

APPENDICES

It is asserted that to deprive the masses of their opportunity
to learn English, the key to social and economic advancement,
would be a most undemocratic step, which would deepen the chasm
that already exists between the common people and those at the
top of the system. Inability to understand the language of
government might leave the ignorant at the mercy of the unscru-
pulous demagogue![1]

---

[1]
    Clifford H. Prator, Language Teaching in the Philippines
Report (Washington, D.C.: United States Educational Foundation
in the Philippines, 1950), p. 20.

CHAPTER I

INTRODUCTION

Mankind today is in immediate and urgent need of a renewed dedication to the dignity and brotherhood of man. To cultivate this oneness of the human race is one of the duties and responsibilities of teachers.

The United States is in a position to demonstrate to the rest of the world that this "Nation of Nations," by utilizing the contributions of all people within its borders, can attain the goal of unity which comes with understanding. Sound understanding can come only through improved communication--one that takes into account the multiplicity of respected language origins underlying the cohesive force of the English language as used in this nation.

There are still too many young citizens of the United States who come to school for the first time knowing only their mother tongue. Included in this group are _some_ members of the Spanish-speaking population. This study was concerned with the teaching of English to this type of Spanish-speaking child.

Need for the Study

The figures show that between five million[1] to six million[2] people in the United States are of Spanish-speaking descent. The Progress Report[3] (five million figure) shows "that the education of this group is dangerously low."

The writer believes that the education of "this group" would not be "dangerously low" if educators were more aware of the importance of Spanish in the teaching of English to "this group."

---

[1] Progress Report: Mexican-American Study Project No. 7. (Los Angeles, California: Division of Research Graduate School of Business Administration, University of California, November, 1966). pp. 4-9.

[2] United States Commission on Civil Rights Staff Paper for Internal Use and Limited Distribution Only Not for Publication-Staff Paper" Spanish-Speaking Peoples," submitted to the United States Commission on Civil Rights, (February 5, 1964). Part III, p. 3.

[3] Progress Report, op. cit., pp. 4-9.

The Problem

The problem of this study was to survey the development of the teaching of English to Spanish-speaking children in the five Southwestern states in general and in Alamosa, Colorado, in particular

The Method

The method was analyticosynthetic and employed extensive and intensive study and use of authoritative works in philosophy, psychology, psychology of learning, and sociology.

The author has drawn upon a lifetime of experience in this kind of work; as a "bicultural bilingual", as a grade school teacher, as a principal of a grade school, as a visiting teacher for the federal government, and as a college teacher—altogether a formal teaching career of almost forty years.

Terms which need defining will be defined where necessary as they are used in context.

Value of Study

It was the hope of the author that this study would reveal weaknesses and strengths of existing programs and that it would underscore the urgent need for more and better foreign language teaching in the primary grades, especially in the area of teaching English to residents and citizens of the United States who are of Spanish descent.

CHAPTER II

HISTORY OF THE PROBLEM

The Spanish-speaking have a proud heritage which began in the New World (the three Americas) long before the sixteenth century. Teaching and learning has always been a necessary process of successful colonization.

> . . . You suddenly remember that we English-speaking Americans occupy only a part of the continent, and that even in this part the Spaniards were here before us . .
> The Pilgrims at Plymouth discovered that Portuguese and Basque fishermen had for years been curing their fish on Cape Cod. The early Virginia explorers were astonished one day to meet a Spanish-speaking Indian on the James River - 40 years before the Virginia Company settled in Jamestown, several Spanish Hesuits had lost their lives in an effort to Christianize the Indians of Chesapeake Bay.[1]

Spanish Christian education of the natives in the Americas was probably one of the motivating forces in the early exploration of the New World. Perhaps, this motive was lost for a time and an attitude of exploitation of the natives became an accepted form of behavior for a time:

> . . . But after Bishop Las Casas had protested this barbarous policy, Cardinal Ximines, as regent, decreed that all Indians be treated as freemen and steps be taken for their civilization and conversion to Christianity. They were to be gathered into settlements where churches and schools could be established for their welfare.
> Various Catholic orders, particularly the Franciscan, began the task of teaching the aborigines the Spanish language, Christian religion, and the practical arts of European civilization. Most significant was the emphasis upon the teaching of music. . . The padres imported organs from Europe, trained choirs and established schools and colleges. As the result of the urging of various parties, Charles V (1551) ordered that there be "founded in the City of Lima, of the Kingdom of Peru, and in the City of Mexico, of New Spain, a University or center of general studies in each respectively." A small fund from the royal treasury was granted those institutions. The opening of

---

[1]

John Dos Passos, "The Spaniards Were Here Before Us," The Readers Digest, Volume 70 (June, 1957), pp. 215-219.

the University of Mexico was delayed until 1553.[2]

Thus, early education in the New World has a Spanish imprint that possibly cannot be erased and therefore should be understood.

In 1960, Santa Fe, the capital of New Mexico, celebrated her 350th birthday.

It is the oldest capital city in the Union, a seat of government for a decade before the Pilgrims landed on Plymouth Rock.

New Mexico was named on the maps as Nuevo Mejico as early as 1565, but was not colonized until 1598, the second permanent colony in what is now the U.S.

. . . the church of San Miguel, the oldest chapel in the U.S. . . . was built . . . by the Franciscans in 1610.[3]

The names of Padre Escalante, who explored Colorado, of Father Junipero Serra, who established a mission at San Francisco, California, were beginning to be known by 1776.[4] As missionary churches were built, education progressed.

Subsequent developments gradually made the Latin American civilization what it is today. From the Rio Grande south to Cape Horn, Catholic culture prevailed. The means utilized first was the Mission system; later, as culture advanced, came the establishment of towns with parish churches and schools. Within the confines of what later became the United States, Missions were established at St. Augustine, Florida; New Orleans, Louisiana; Laredo, Texas; and in New Mexico and California.[5]

The northern part of New Mexico is at the southernmost part of Colorado. It is at this at this point, on the site of the Beaubien

---

[2]

Frederick Eby, The Development of Modern Education (New York: Prentice-Hall, Inc., 1952), p. 227.

[3]

Chris Rollman, "Santa Fe: City of Faith." The Catholic Digest, (September, 1960), pp. 26-32.

[4]

Paul H. Hallett, "Film Shows Exploration in Colorado by Pioneers," The Southern Colorado Register (Friday, July 17, 1962).

[5]

Eby, Op. cit., p. 227.

Land Grant, that the first white settlement in Colorado, San Luis, was established by eleven Spanish-speaking men in 1851. It was in 1852 that the men brought their wives and families from Taos, Santa Fe, San Juan, and Abique, New Mexico.[6] The following quote is true of the people of the San Luis Valley as it is of the people of northern New Mexico:

> The Spanish-speaking people of New Mexico particularly in the northern part, are known as Spanish-American. They are descended from the early Spanish colonials and have never had a strong feeling that Mexico is their mother country. On the contrary, they were shut off from Mexico City by vast distances of barren lands which lessened cultural intermingling. They had political and economic powers from Spain.[7]

Spanish settlements gathered strength and popularity when the Conejos Grant was started in 1853-1854. The two settlements were known to each other. From these two, stockmen and farmers moved to La Loma, Carnero, and Saguache. From then on, the San Luis Valley definitely had three centers of culture: the Conejos area in the southwest, the San Luis area in the southeast, and the Saguache area in the northwest. Today, Alamosa is found approximately in the center of what used to be the three culture centers of the San Luis Valley. Until the "early seventies"[8] when the first Nordic whites entered the Valley, the Spanish culture remained intact. Early English-speaking settlers referred to the people they found in the Valley as Mexicans (possibly because the people had come from New Mexico) and the term is still occasionally used.

When the United States army occupied Santa Fe in 1846, the New Mexican began to feel the need of knowing English. The "problem" of teaching English to Spanish-speaking persons has long been recognized, directly in New Mexico and indirectly in Colorado. Through the close ties between the first settlers of Colorado and the more established settlers of New Mexico, teaching materials and knowledge have been shared. For this reason, this study will refer to relevant early educational approaches that came from New Mexico. In 1851 English, taught by a native speaker, was made available to Spanish-speaking students:

---

[6]
Delfino Salazar. Personal interview. Institute of Arts and Crafts, San Luis, Colorado, March, 1946.

[7]
L.S. Tireman, Teaching Spanish-Speaking Children (Albuquerque: University of New Mexico Press, 1951), p. 14.

[8]
Frank C. Spencer, The Story of the San Luis Valley (Denver: The World Press, Inc., 1924), p. 72.

El ano de 1851, cuando ya hubo su Senoria Lamy allanado las dificultades que se le presentaban a su llegado die el primer paso para introducir una escuela en Nuevo Mexico con el objeto de ensenar el Ingles; hizo venir un profesor de habla Ingles llamado E. Noel . . .

En 1852, se establecio en Santa Fe la segundo escuela privada en la que se ensenaba la idioma Ingles . . . pero habia al mismo tiempo otra escuela publica, que conducia un maestro llamado Pacheco.[9]

Dr. L.S. Tireman quotes the Estatuas de Nuevo Mexico to show that both English and Spanish proficiency was sought from educators teaching in the State's Normal Schools.[10]

With the waning of Spanish power in the Americas, with the establishment of the United States independence, and with the granting of statehood to the southwestern states (Arizona, California, Colorado, New Mexico, and Texas), the influence of the English language and the English culture gathered momentum in the New World. The mastery of the English language began to be imperative for those few who recognized the change and who desired to advance in the new situation. The majority of the people did not for some time to come realize the implications of the change. "Geographical isolation among the native American stock is most notable in isolated mountain areas."[11]

The San Luis Valley, located in the southern part of Colorado, surrounded by mountains on three sides and ranging in altitude from 7500-8500 feet, is 120 miles long and averages 40 miles in width.[12] The "geographical isolation" of the Spanish-speaking group in the San Luis Valley has kept alive and flourishing 15th-16th century Spanish up to the present time.

There is no need, at this time, to go into a detailed account of

---

[9]
E. Lic. Benjamin M. Read, Historia Illustrada De Nuevo Mexico (Santa Fe, New Mexico: Compania Impresora Del Nuevo Mexico, 1951), p. 345.

[10]
Tireman, op. cit., pp. 76-77.

[11]
Paul H. Landis, Rural Life in Progress (New York: McGraw-Hill Publishing Company, 1940), pp. 169-170.

[12]
Spencer, op. cit., p. 5.

the initial struggles and hardships which Spanish-speaking parents encountered when they tried to place their children in English-speaking schools. An unpublished master's thesis presents a detailed account of these initial obstacles. Suffice it to say that it was not easy then and to some it is still not easy today to attend English-speaking schools.[13]

Two world wars, a cold war or two and the threat of a third world war have focused attention on the dangers inherent in the lack of communication among large groups of people within the United States. More and more effort is being expended in providing expert assistance in the expansion of educational opportunities to so-called "culturally deprived" in an English-speaking, middle-class, Protestant nation, but they themselves have a culture and it may be that they have a contribution to make to the dominant group that up to now has not been fully acknowledged.

The San Jose Experimental School[14] was one of the first sophisticated attempts to identify the needs and to improve the instruction of Spanish-speaking pupils in the southwest. It was initiated in September, 1930, through the combined efforts of the University of New Mexico, the New Mexico State Board of Education, the late U.S. Senator Bronson M. Cutting, the Bernalillo County Board of Education, and the General Education Board. The results have been published in a small book.[15] After 1930 there were more and more printed materials available for teachers and more interest shown in the problem.[16]

13
    Eva R. Borrego, "Some Educational Aspects Affecting Acculturation of The Spanish-Culture Background Student in the San Luis Valley" (unpublished Master's thesis, Adams State College, Alamosa, Colorado, 1946).

14
    "The San Jose Training School," The University of New Mexico Bulletin, Training School Series, Vol. 1, No. 1, (October, 1930).

15
    _____. We Learn English, San Jose Experimental School (Albuquerque, New Mexico: University of New Mexico Press, 1936).

16
    Marie Hughes, Teaching a Standard English Vocabulary With Initial Reading Instruction (New Mexico: Issued by State Department of Education, 1936); H.T. Manuel, The Education of Mexican and Spanish-speaking Children in Texas (Austin: The University of Texas Press, 1930); _____, Learning English Incidentally: A Study of Bilingual Children, Bulletin 1937, No. 15, U.S. Dept. of Interior, Office of Education, Project Research in Universities (Washington, D.C.: Government Printing Office, 1938); Jean Piaget, La langue et la pensee Chez l'enfant (Neuchatel: Delachaux et Niestle, 1924-5), trans. The Language and Thought of the Child (New York: Harcourt, Brace, 1932).

The 1948 Colorado Course of Study[17] has a section on the teaching of the bilingual. The Curriculum Guide for Elementary Schools in New Mexico, 1950,[18] also has a fine section titled, "Non-English Speaking Children." The Course of Study for Elementary Schools of Arizona, 1939,[19] has a special Bulletin (13) concerned with "Instruction of Bilingual Children." The State of California in 1932 put out a Department of Education Bulletin,[20] A Guide for Teachers of Beginning Non-English Speaking Children. A Bibliography: Materials Relating to the Education of Spanish-Speaking People[21] was the University of Texas Press contribution in 1948. Southwest Texas State Teachers College had an interesting little booklet.[22]

This writer believes that the United States is "resolving this contradiction between creed and practice" better than any other country in the world. But, today the temper of the many underprivileged people is slipping its bounds. The United States must be keenly aware of what is at stake and move faster in this race "against catastrophe" by better handling of this contradiction.

This contradiction between creed and practice must once and for all be resolved. If we mean what we say by equality and brotherhood, we cannot rest until people of different colors,

---

17
    The Colorado Course of Study, 1948.

18
    Charles E. Rose (Superintendent of Public Instruction), Curriculum Guide for Elementary Schools in New Mexico (Santa Fe, New Mexico: State Department of Education, 1950.)

19
    H.E. Hendrix (State Superintendent), Course of Study for Elementary Schools of Arizona, Bulletin Number Thirteen, "Instruction of Bilingual Children" (Phoenix, Arizona: State Department of Education, 1939).

20
    Helen Hefferman (chief), A Guide for Teachers of Beginning Non-English Speaking Children (Sacramento: California State Printing Office, 1932).

21
    Clarice T. Whittenburg and George I. Sanchez, Materials Relating to the Education of Spanish-Speaking People: A Bibliography (Austin: The University of Texas Press, 1948.

22
    Willa Vaughn Tinsley (ed.), Music Activities for Latin-American Children in the Elementary Grades (San Marcos, Texas: Southwest Texas Teachers College, 1944).

religions, and nationalities have full privileges of economic opportunity and citizenship in the democratic community.[23]

Many of these early publications have exhibited a genuine concern and a sympathetic understanding of the problem. Many of these have valuable usable information. Old material is not necessarily useless. It is true that much has since been learned concerning children and how they learn, much has been experimentally discovered about the role of language, and the process of becoming adults, but the sound basic foundation laid by the pioneers in this work should not be discounted. True progress, in any area, comes through the selection and use of the best of the past and the best of the new. It is in this selection that bias and prejudice have no place; it is here that the ones who do the selecting must keep in mind the dignity and brotherhood of man; it is here that the role of opportunity in the lives of all must be more than a creed.

Dr. L.S. Tireman, in his book Teaching Spanish-Speaking Children,[24] has reviewed the teaching of English to children in a clear concise fashion. His material shows how programs in other "bilingual" nations have progressed. He mentions Puerto Rico, Wales, Belgium, Luxemburg, Northern Canada, and South Africa; then he concentrates on New Mexico and the Spanish-speaking learner of English. This book emphasizes the fact that "bilingualism" is not a new phenomenon and that it is a continuing one. Subsequent world happenings seem to indicate that denying "mother" languages to vast numbers of people is not a wise procedure. Misunderstandings among nations can arise out of lack of communication in a particular language, but there is a language that often could be utilized and is not; The Silent Language[25] of action, of behavior, of sensitivity, and love of fellowmen. The teaching of a new language to one already knowing a language which will result in a "bilingual" should not imply the erasing of the native language.

Figures show that the number of Spanish-speaking people in the United States is constantly growing. There has been an increase in the southwest alone:

White persons of Spanish surname in the U.S. Southwest,

23

Theodore Brameld, "Intercultural Democracy--Education's New Frontier," The Educational Forum, Vol. XII, November, 1947.

24

Tireman, op. cit.

25

Edward T. Hall, The Silent Language (Greenwich, Conn.: Fawcett Publications, Inc., 1963).

where the Mexican-American population is concentrated, numbered 3,465,000, according to 1960 Census of Population figures announced by the Bureau of the Census, U.S. Department of Commerce. This was an increase of 1,175,450, or 51.3 per cent over the figure reported in the 1950 Census of Population.[26]

Puerto Ricans in New York and New Jersey numbered 697,973, and in Florida 19,535. These figures did not show the number of Puerto Ricans for the Southwest States.[27] The influx of Cubans to Florida apparently is not tabulated in the 1960 census report.

In a new Staff Paper[28] which as yet has not been released for publication, the following figure is found, "there are six million Spanish-speaking people in the United States and their number is growing." Many of the members of this six million are called migrants---meaning that they are United States citizens who are agricultural workers and follow one of the "five major annual streams"[29] that originate in the southern states.

There are somewhere near two million migrant workers in the United States; the education of their children is a matter of ever increasing importance. The socio-economic problems faced by our nation in dealing with the migrants' situation are complex. These problems must be studied carefully and in depth if they are to be solved.[30]

26
Luther H. Hodges, Secretary, "White Persons of Spanish Surname," Census: For Release June 3, 1962, (Washington, D.C.: United States Department of Commerce, June 3, 1962), 11 single sheets.

27
Ibid.

28
United States Commission on Civil Rights Staff Paper for Internal Use and Limited Distribution Only Not for Publication - Staff Paper, op. cit., p. 3.

29
James E. Peiffer, Cultural Background of Americans of Mexican Descent (Toledo, Ohio: Toledo Diocesan Councils of Catholic Men and Women, 1962), pp. 3-20.

30
Byron W. Hansford, Commissioner of Education in Colorado, Guide to Organization and Administration of Migrant Education Programs: An Aid for the Implementation of Educational Opportunities for Children of Migratory Agricultural People (Denver: Colorado State Department of Education, 1963), pp. 3-10.

The above quotation came from a bulletin which was developed at an Adams State College Workshop on Migrant Education in the summer of 1962. This bulletin has some very fine instructional information, an excellent bibliography, and a tremendous list of contact groups for local, state, and national cooperative action. Migrants may be other than Spanish-speaking, but the main group considered at this particular workshop was the Spanish-speaking group.

The statement is often heard from some educators and writers who work with the Spanish-speaking newly come from Mexico, "But they are different, they are of a lower class of people!" The author's answer to this is, "How do you know?" These people are defenseless, exploited, and "forgotten". How can anyone know whether they are incapable of learning if the opportunity to learn under favorable conditions is denied them?

> Large numbers of people native to Mexico are coming to the United States each year. In 1960 alone, thirty-three thousand Mexican Nationals legally entered the United States with intentions of residing here permanently. They are settling in all parts of the country, parts that a few years ago never saw a Mexican.
>
> When people of Mexican descent come into a particular area they often become the victims of misunderstandings and prejudice. They are looked upon by the rest of the community as strange and not to be trusted. They speak a strange language and have strange and often unpopular habits and attitudes. . . They band together in little groups, cut off from others. This situation results in an even greater wall of ignorance being thrown up between them and the community.[31]

There are enough people involved in this matter of learning English as a foreign language initially, to make it the business of every individual in the United States. It might make the native speaker of English even a better speaker. The United States is a great country because so many cultures have contributed to its greatness. There is still an untapped potential in these cultures that can, through the adopted sons of the nation, continue to give impetus to this greatness. The potential locked up within the Spanish-speaking citizens can be released only by providing them with the main tool, the ability to communicate. This means the ability to handle the English language adequately.

A nation is great only because its people are on the move together, each member recognizing the worth of every other. This is the image

---

[31]

    Peiffer, op. cit., p. 3.

that the United States should aspire to with all the "know-how" at its disposal.

In 1925, "New Horizons" opened to Spanish-speaking young men and women in Southern Colorado. This was the call to higher education provided by Adams State College. The first President, Ira Richardson, had the vision of truly extending a welcome to all students. A college in Alamosa meant that it was available; it was there. The cost was kept at a minimum and the psychological climate was favorable. As this high incentive became known to the Spanish-speaking, staying in school and graduating from high school became a little more attractive. It was still not too attractive because a few of the early and courageous students who did go to college (and some did graduate) found that they could not find jobs. But, more and more young people came; the early graduates led the way; many began to find jobs; education began to be important to this group of people. It is true that in the beginning the only jobs available were in Spanish-speaking communities or out of the state. This kind of job discrimination actually helped the Spanish-speaking because their schools began to have better qualified teachers. These first alumni of Adams State College inspired many others of their own group to continue their education and another barrier went down.

In November of 1943, Adams State College opened the Institute of Arts and Crafts in San Luis, Colorado, just twenty-five miles east and sixteen miles south of Alamosa and again education came to the people of Spanish-speaking descent. The author once had an article published which gave this adventure into teaching and learning a modest introduction. Because it has a direct bearing on the building of a desire to learn English in the hearts of people, this article is included here in its entirety:

Through the San Luis Institute
Life Takes on New Meaning

Adams State College Takes Over Building Built by WPA for a Community Center and Sets Up Course of Study Designed to Raise Standard of Living for an Entire Community.

The Institute of Arts and Crafts, a branch of Adams State College, is located 25 miles east and 16 miles south of Alamosa in the oldest town of Colorado, San Luis. The town of San Luis is the center of a Spanish culture which is still strongly motivated and influenced by the Spanish pattern and design for living.

A WPA building, originally constructed for a community center, was given to Adams State College by the community with the understanding that the college administration would bring and make higher education available to the people of San Luis. In two weeks, the Institute of Arts

12

and Crafts was in operation with 11 students and three instructors. Thus, in November, 1943, the Institute of Arts and Crafts was introduced by request to the community.

In February, Miss Achsa Nash, who was doing some special work for the U.S. Office of Education, joined the staff as a part time instructor. I joined the staff in September, 1944. The enrollment was 30, counting the part time inservice teacher students. In 1945, two more instructors were added and our enrollment rose to 33.

The G.I. Bill of Rights made the vocational-educational set-up possible in January, 1946. Our initial enrollment was six.

Eleven Full-Time Instructors

In the spring quarter of 1950 our enrollment was 150 in general vocation; 39, regular college full time; 22, regular college part time (inservice); and 36 in on-the-farm training, a total of 247. We have a staff of 11 on the campus; two other instructors come in three nights a week on the farm program. Our facilities consist of eight classrooms, a small library, reading room auditorium, circulating library, curriculum laboratory, and a shop. We use student clerical help and student janitor service. Our conveniences are limited.

Any success which we have had in helping our community to help itself has been possible only through the cooperation of the parents, public spirited citizens, teachers, students, and the county superintendent.

The Institute of Arts and Crafts has a two-year teacher training course which stresses rural work. The students take an intensive and wide-ranged two-year work period with the objective of rural work in mind. The students understand and are fully aware of their responsibilities as future constructive community leaders. At the end of the two-year course, our students may receive the Associate Arts degree and start teaching or continue working on their A.B. degree in another institution of higher learning.

The teacher already in the field has the opportunity to take part time work at the Institute, to use the facilities there, and to seek aid from the faculty members. The curriculum laboratory is available for construction of teaching aids which the teacher may wish to make.

The circulating library is made up of complete sets (30 to 40) of textbooks in many fields of subject matter. These books have been given to the Institute by administrators of the

Monte Vista, Alamosa, and Sargent elementary schools as they buy the newer and more modern sets. The books are in fine shape and certainly of immense value to the group. The Denver Junior League sent a wonderful collection of story books that have given joy to many youngsters. Other interested people have given us books from time to time and now we have 6,000 available. Last week 2,000 were out in the field being used.

Institute Becomes Health Center

Soon after the opening of the Institute of Arts and Crafts a San Luis doctor died, leaving the community with no medical help at all. The nearest hospital in Alamosa was almost too far away to be of practical use to most people. The faculty at the Institute began a series of health knowledge programs. George Gates from the American Red Cross was available for first aid courses and Miss Lorensen from the Red Cross taught nutrition courses.

Films on health were shown throughout the country wherever electric current was available. Institute students took an active part in the showing of the films, particularly the tuberculosis films which were explained in Spanish to the people requesting them in that language. The school children all saw "Prepare for Invasion," a film on immunization. Later when Mrs. Marvella Smith, head of the San Luis Welfare Office, telephoned the Institute personnel asking for help in a diptheria emergency, the whole community mobilized for action and about 1,300 children were immunized. The people from the State Health Department, headed by Mrs. Bowdin, responded beautifully.

Mr. Fred Worman, Adams State College, working with the U.S. Navy, tried out a new medication for the skin disease, impetigo. Using student help, he worked for two years at this problem with the following result: the first year, 306 cases were treated; second year, 96; third year, 25; fourth year, one; and the next two years, none. After the first two years, Mr. Worman did not need to come down to do the work; the parents, teachers and children had learned to do what was necessary to keep well.

Dr. Elizabeth Gernes spent some time in San Luis working with the county teachers. She visited a great deal and taught a class at the Institute which developed a very fine bulletin called "Practical Health Problems in Education." Later, during a summer session at Adams State College, she developed another bulletin called "Community Resources."

Emphasis on Use of English

One of the greatest contributions of the Institute of Arts and Crafts to the people of Costilla County was the emphasis on the use of the English language throughout the county. The school children have had more of a desire and an opportunity to use the English language. Young qualified teachers, who expect and demand an understanding use of the English language, have worked a great change in the community's attitudes toward all educational progress. A feeling of belonging and of being a part of a great whole is being experienced.

New feelings toward the democratic way of life are being demonstrated. The gap existing between cultures is being closed. Care is being exercised in preserving the best of the old culture and a great attempt is being made to gain the best of the new culture.

The San Luis Art Club, composed mainly of townspeople, has been an active and forceful group. It encourages creative work and provides a satisfactory outlet for pent-up emotions. The group meets every Wednesday, some members using the crafts room, others using the shop. A faculty advisor is always available. Several home art exhibits have been held; a great social ball is held every year, and creative art contests among the school children have been conducted by the art club members. This group also donated the money for the redecoration of the auditorium. The Friends of Art, a state organization, is sponsored by this club also.

Sixty-Two Teachers in County

Costilla County employs 62 teachers, of whom 48 have had work at Adams State College, and 14 are now taking inservice college work there. We have eight teachers with A.B. degrees teaching in the county and five of these started at the Institute. Two of our former students are working for masters' degrees.

The vocational-educational set-up helps 186 ex-G.I.'s to better, richer living in farm accounting, farm problems, farm knowledges, citizenship, history, English, reading, and current events. Films are utilized to a great extent with these men.

The shop provides opportunity for skilled work in furniture making and repair, machine repair (tractors, autos, rakes, etc.), and it is a popular place. Incidental learnings, such as safety, courtesy, and perseverance are noted.

These men participate in social activities. Their wives enjoy our formal parties, picnics and get-togethers. The library facilities are used a great deal by these men.

Attending assembly programs and watching the associated students and faculty operate have given these men an insight into college life and education in general that has changed their attitude toward modern society and life as it exists.

We did have a construction-vocational set up and during its existence a duplex was built. Two workers became skilled and at least 20 learned the fundamentals of building.

Many of the community groups use the Institute building as a center meeting place. Practically every night all classrooms are in use, and the following groups may be meeting: civil air patrol, Izaac Walton, Knights of Columbus, band beginners, old-timers' baseball league, square dancing group, Newman club, glee club and town open meeting groups. The auditorium chairs are used by community members for wakes and weddings. People come in for information and help, and no one is turned away.

A foundation is being laid at the Institute of Arts and Crafts that will be far-reaching in its effect. It cannot be measured because individuals are finding satisfaction in living that they had never experienced before.[32]

More recently, Colorado has led the way in migrant education.

The Colorado State Department of Education and Adams State College have long been interested in the problems of migrant education. They have cooperated in this area for many years, most notably through joint sponsorship of summer workshops. . . . For eight years also the State of Colorado has underwritten the cost of a number of special summer programs designed specifically to help these boys and girls.[33]

The first Bilingual Workshop took place at Adams State College in 1954 and resulted in a ditto copy; the next one in 1957, more elaborate,

---

[32]
    Eva R. Borrego, "Through the San Luis Institute Life Takes on New Meaning," Rural Life and Education in the Rocky Mountain Empire (Denver: Division of Publications, The Colorado Education Association, 1950), pp. 13, 14-17.

[33]
    Hansford, op. cit., pp. 1-2.

was published by the Colorado State Department of Education. The 1962 Workshop, again, dealt with problems of people who have difficulty communicating. The summer of 1964 Workshop was concerned with the Teaching of English as a Second Language and included the vast Indian population.

The "special summer programs" started in 1955, when the first pilot summer school was set up at Wiggins. Probably the greatest encouragement to this type of program came through the passing by the Colorado General Assembly of the Migrant Children Education Act.[34] Other pilot schools were established in Palisade, Fort Lupton, Rocky Ford, Monte Vista, and Sierra Grande. Monte Vista and Sierra Grande are both in the San Luis Valley.

On June 24, 1964, the first of three workshops dealing with the "Teaching of English as a Second Language"[35] was held at Security, Colorado. This research project, sponsored by the State Department of Education and financially aided by the federal government was given the number "2734" (Colorado). It was one of twenty-eight different projects across the nation. Nearly one million dollars was expended during eighteen months. The purpose was a concentrated effort toward the improvement of first grade reading. The project produced some very substantial "scientific" evidence for many of the suggestions and educational offerings found in "old" bulletins, periodicals, and courses of study that have not been sufficiently digested and practiced. The author is not belittling the "scientific" approach, she is just pointing out the "good that is often buried" in the archives.

During the summer of 1967, the writer together with Dr. Philip Rowley of the Center for Cultural Studies at Adams State College, conducted a workshop structured on the following pages of 18, 19, 20, 21, 22, 23 and 24.

All over the United States dedicated people are working, trying to find the best solution to this problem.

Nine state citizens' committees exist at present. These are found in Colorado, Illinois, Indiana, Michigan, New York, Oregon, Pennsylvania, Washington and Wisconsin. . . . The Pennsylvania Citizens Committee, which is the oldest, is given credit for helping that state in initiating its program of day-care centers, now financed by the government,

---

34

The Colorado Program for the Education of Migrant Children, Introduction (Denver: State Department of Education, June 14, 1961), pp. 1-11.

35

Roy M. McCanne: Project 2734 (Denver: Colorado State Department of Education, 1964), pp. 1-19.

Workshop

Adams State College

July 17-18

Industrial Arts

Building 110

Prepared

by

Eva R. Borrego

18

Approaches

I. Teaching English to Spanish-Speaking

   Teaching Spanish to English-Speaking

   First-Class Citizens
        knowing and appreciating Two Languages

II. Clarifying the Concepts of:

                    The Haves

                    The Havenots

```
Target..............................Attitudes
                                    Strengthened and Enriched


Emphasis............................Cultural Implications


Implementation......................Practical materials,
                                    devices, sources,
                                    activities, etc.


Outcome.............................Advantaged and Privileged
                                    Education For All.
```

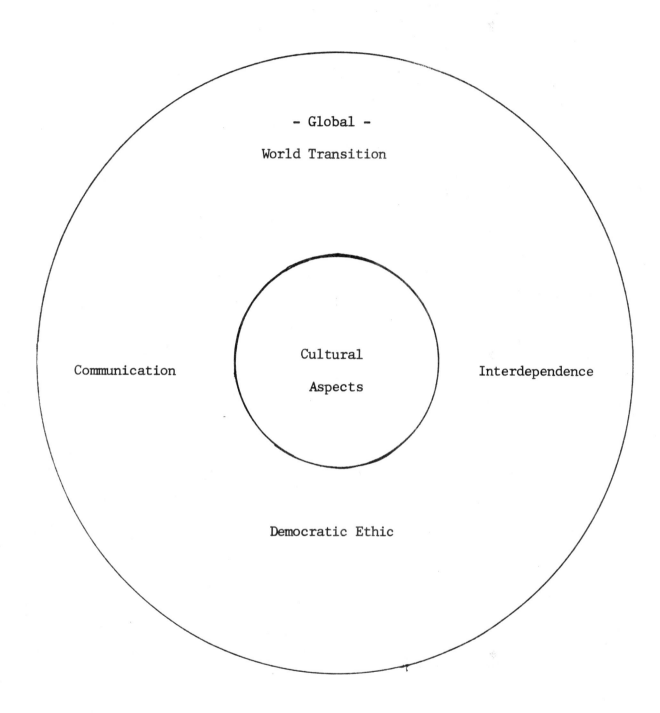

- Global -

World Transition

Communication

Cultural

Aspects

Interdependence

Democratic Ethic

Change in Attitudes

21

Basic Texts

McRae, Margit   Teaching Spanish
                                 In the Grades

Zintz, Miles   Education Across
                                 Cultures

Frost and Hawkes   The Disadvantaged
                                 Child

(Suggested)

Source Material

The

Center for Cultural

Studies

Advantaged And Privileged Education

For All

2:00 - 3:00	Welcome Address
3:00 - 4:00	Coffee
4:00 - 5:00	Organizational Activity

_____

_____

_____

_____

_____

_____

and for helping in passing legislation for summer schools.[36]

These citizens' committees have worked hard to alleviate the condition of many of the Spanish-speaking population whose plight, in a very real sense, is the result of not knowing English. Other states have conducted workshops and have published papers, bulletins, supplements to courses of study, and books.[37]

The number of children who have not yet lifted the "language curtain" in the United States is still too great; the ignorance of some teachers concerning this danger is still too much; the possible exposure of enemy idealogies to this group becomes more real every day. Thus, for educators, there can be no relaxation even for one moment, in their fight for education of full, informed, and participating citizens in a democracy.

Whether the Spanish-speaking student is a migrant child or whether he is a permanent citizen of a community, the problem of learning English is the paramount one. This is the challenge to Master Teachers today in the United States.

36
Hansford, op. cit., p. 13.

37
Theodore Huebener, Maey Finocchiaro, English for Spanish-Americans (New York: Henry Holt and Company, 1950), pp. 411; Walter G. Martin (Supt.), Teaching Children Who Move with the Crops (Fresno, California: The Educational Program for Migrant Children, 1956), pp. 95; Jack Cohn, "The Integration of Spanish-Speaking Newcomers in a 'Fringe Area' School," The National Elementary Principal, Vol. XXXIX, No. 6, May, 1960; John H. Swenson, Learning on the Move: A Guide for Migrant Education (Denver: Colorado State Department of Education, 1960), pp. 220; E. Roby Leighton (ed.), Workshop for Teachers of Bilingual Students (Phoenix, Arizona: University of Arizona, College of Education, 1961), p. 115; Helen Harter, English is Fun or The Rhythm and Song Approach to the Teaching of English to Non-English Speaking Beginners, Second Edition (Tempe, Arizona: Helen Harter, 1962), pp. 82; _____ Program for Non-English Speaking Beginners. revised (Las Cruces, New Mexico: Las Cruces Schools, 1963), pp. 29; Teachers Guide to the Education of Spanish-Speaking Children, Staff in Elementary Education (Sacramento: California State Department of Education, Vol. XXI, No. 14, 1952), pp. 37-62.

CHAPTER III

A MASTER TEACHER

It is possible today to offer schools and school personnel the most up-to-date and the most efficient facilities, equipment, materials, and plants that have ever been devised by men. In many areas, it is an established fact that more and more students are attending classes for longer and longer periods of time. The number of students graduating from high schools and colleges is constantly increasing. Revision of teacher-preparation criteria propels and demands higher and higher degrees. The costs of education keep pace with the degrees. All of this provides a proud and comforting image of education in the United States.

But, like an iceberg, the educational block has a submerged mass that is almost invisible, barely acknowledged, and all but forgotten. Many of our "fine" citizens are not aware that this mass exists. Sad to say, many educators do not care that it exists, are impatient with this "legend," or are jumping on the bandwagon of "crash programs" without proper planning or provision.

It follows, then, that some of our young, eager, academically able prospective teachers fall into the blindness of complacency and the status quo. It is to be hoped that each teacher serving the schools of this country should aspire to be a master teacher, who is versed in a rich, professional background of general and specific education, armed with an historically rooted philosophy, deeply aware of world affairs and challenged by the "melting-pot" nature of the United States with its kaleidoscopic process of acculturation and enculturation.[1]

To take off the blinders of satisfaction requires a cold plunge

---

[1]
Ruth Benedict, Patterns of Culture (New York: The New American Library of World Literature, Inc., 1960, A New Mentor Book), pp. 1-254; Eva R. Borrego, Some Educational Aspects Affecting Acculturation of the Spanish-Culture Background Student in the San Luis Valley. Unpublished Master's Thesis, Alamosa, Colorado, Adams State College, 1946, pp. 1-61; Ina Corrine Brown, Understanding Other Cultures (Englewood Cliffs, New Jersey: Prentice-Hall, Inc., 1963), pp. 1-175; Edward T. Hall, The Silent Language, op. cit., pp. 1-182; Herschel T. Manuel, Spanish-Speaking Children of the Southwest: Their Education and the Public Welfare (Austin, Texas: University of Texas Press, 1965), pp. 1-207; Miles V. Zintz, Education Across Cultures (Dubuque, Iowa: Wm. C. Brown Book Company, 1963), pp. 1-362.

below the surface of what previously had formed the image. The submerged factors[2] will take on substance[3] and master teachers will form new and useful <u>attitudes</u>[4] which will enable them to teach more successfully the up to now unseen mass.

Poor people compose this unseen and forgotten <u>mass</u>. Their problems are legion; their hopes are few. Of all the poor, frustrated people below the high standard of living <u>image</u> of the United States, one group is selected, now, to present to the master teacher. This is the Spanish-speaking group not yet able to speak English. This group needs desperately to acquire this ability so that it can move into the existing so-called culture as interpreted by the upper part of the educational iceberg........more about this later.

The author of this paper holds no brief for specialization to the point of fragmentation. A master teacher in a proper teacher-pupil ratio situation, with an adequate amount of concentrated precise coaching in a special or specific confrontation, should be able to teach anyone. It is in this area of confrontation that the attitudinal posture of the teacher can either work seeming miracles or cause downright tragedies. "A teacher is perhaps more to be judged by his effect on students' attitudes than by any other learning....."[5]

If the teacher is to have an "effect on students' attitudes", the teacher himself must have the kind of attitudes that will constructively help them.

A common failing of schools is to save all praise for those few pupils who are most conspicuously successful. . .
Characteristically two-thirds of the student body go through school without being known personally to the bulk of their

---

2
Harold W. Bernard, Psychology of Learning and Teaching, Second Edition (New York: McGraw-Hill Book Company, 1965), p. 326.

3
Theodore Brameld, Education for the Emerging Age: Newer Ends and Stronger Means, Foreword by Robert Ulick (New York: Harper and Row Publishers, 1965), p. 77.

4
Cole S. Brembeck, Social Foundations of Education: A Cross-Cultural Approach (New York: John Wiley and Sons, Inc., 1966), pp. 175-200.

5
Lee J. Cronback, Educational Psychology (New York: Harcourt, Brace and Co., 1954), p. 325.

classmates or to their teachers.[6]

The rest of this chapter is devoted to selected materials posing concepts which hopefully should help develop the kind of attitudes and the necessary insights for skilled workmanship necessary for the master teacher's proper growth and development.

One more word, with full cognizance of the usefulness of new methods and devices: the master teacher will take it for granted that he will WORK. It is so easy in this day of mechanization, of programmed texts, of group processes, and of the belief in learning by experience to put the burden of teaching on the students themselves. It is true that students learn by themselves--"No man can understand anything for another"--but, the teacher is the "cause" of student's desire to do it.

> The teacher has this advantage over most other persons in
> the world; he is expected to be concerned with the truth
> and nothing but the truth, and for its own sake. . . This
> is a precious advantage and a priceless privilege.[7]

The teacher is duty bound to value this "precious advantage . . . this priceless privilege . . ." As a seeker of truth, the teacher must ever be a student, who in sincerely searching for truth, invariably finds a measure of wisdom.

Much of this truth and wisdom will deal with a satisfyingly clear concept of the nature of the learner for this knowledge is basic to the educational process. If the student is accepted as a "beast", as a "noble savage", as a "shopper", as a "shaper",[8] or as a god who needs no God, he will be taught according to his acceptance.

As the nature of man is studied by the prospective teacher, psychology and all other behavioral sciences should be consulted. If an emphasis is sought, it would be in cultural aspects of humanity and

---

6

Ibid., p. 572.

7

Mark Van Doren, "Seekers After Truth," in D. Louis Sharpe (ed.) Why Teach (New York: Henry Holt and Company, 1957), p. 229.

8

Charles J. Brauner and Robert W. Burns, Problems in Education and Philosophy, Foundation of Education Series (Englewood Cliffs, New Jersey: Prentice-Hall, 1965), pp. 133-152.

not in the cold factual "unfinished science"[9] called psychology.

The teacher's quest of a sensitive and as complete as possible understanding of the student will be a life-long concern. A master teacher does not limit his efforts to helping only a highly intellectual organism evolve:

> ... I shall tell you immediately that a true scholar is essentially a man whose intellectual life is part and parcel of his moral life; in other words, a scholar is a man who has decided, once and for all, to carry all the requirements of his moral consciousness into his intellectual life ... intellectual honesty is a scrupulous respect for truth.[10]

Robert Ulich comments on this quality of man as follows:

> ... But even in the classroom of a primary school forms of thinking are carried on that are independent of environmental factors. The fundamentals of arithmetic, for example, were as true under Alexander the Great as they are today and will be tomorrow. We recognize universal logical axioms and follow rules of reasoning which, from my point of view, apply also to questions of moral conduct. This influence of intellect on the affairs of man and its indomitable cogency explain why tyrants and despots cannot long survive in an enlightened society. Whence these rules come, we do not know. Alas! The attempt at an answer would lead us into metaphysics, and that is an unpopular field among educators. Nevertheless, the rules exist.[11]

Again, Robert Ulich states his concept of the origin of man's strength and the source of his essence (higher in quality than a mere

---

9

Floyd L. Ruch, Psychology and Life, Sixth Edition (Chicago: Scott, Foresman and Company, 1963), p. 3.

10

Etienne Gilson, A Gilson Reader: Selections from the Writings of Etienne Gilson, Edited, with an Introduction by Anton C. Pegis (Garden City, New York: Image Books, a Division of Doubleday & Company, Inc., 1957), p. 26.

11

Robert Ulich, "Foreword," Education For the Emerging Age: Newer Ends and Stronger Means (New York: Harper & Row, Publishers, 1965), p. 4iii.

organism):

> . . . We are justified in supposing that our ethical behavior
> has its origin not in arbitrary human decisions in isolated
> desires--such as the will to power, competition or fears on
> the one hand, or man's spiritual and ideal products of the
> mind on the other hand--but in ultimate energies which work
> at the bottom of total existence.[12]

The "eminent dignity" of teaching should be fully understood by
the teacher, not by seeking material status, but by accepting the tremendous responsibility which the following quotations indicate:

> . . . Perhaps only the shock of discovery that humanity is
> confronted with the prospect of chaos--if not total destruc-
> tion--can now arouse education.[13]

> . . . Powerful tools are in the process of being forged by
> the scientists who study man as a social animal . . .
> These tools can be used to further or to destroy certain
> types of behavior and certain social patterns.[14]

Today, more than ever, teachers are key figures in the forging of
a new society in a technological world, an uncertain, anxious world.

Although adults may be "alienated", fearful, "angry", and blase,
they should not deprive the young of their right to be hopeful, imagin-
ative, trusting, and brave. It may very well come to be that teachers,
in the future, will have to stand up and be counted as they protect the
children from exploitation by adults who mistakenly impose on the young
their own adult views and dis-illusionments. Children have a right to
their illusions and to their fanciful wonderworld.

Initially, education has always dealt with the young.[15] No matter
what the surroundings are in time and space, the new life must pursue

---

[12]
Robert Ulich, Philosophy of Education (New York: American Book
Company, 1961), pp. 53-54.

[13]
Brameld, op. cit., p. 14.

[14]
J.B. Conant, Science and Common Sense (New Haven: Yale University
Press, 1951), p. 345.

[15]
Brembeck, op. cit., p. 9.

the long journey of growth and development in its own particular style. Its own potential is present and clamors for fulfillment. The matter of timing is one of the secrets of master teaching. There is a pattern to the student's life movement and the multiplicity of intricate, coordinated and related designs taking shape in infinite variety within this mystery of person that demands the most patient and careful, time-consuming and sensitive support. This support should come from all adults because all adults teach.

No one is ever born really knowing, but everyone is capable in some degree to know. This is the task of the teacher to help learners know. The rare moment of discovery and of knowing is perhaps due to the radiation and warmth from one human being to another. This is the essence which is denied to automation and mechanized teaching. This is the happiness reserved to teachers who have caused the moment.

The great emphasis given to self-realization or self-fulfillment at every level in our society today needs to be analyzed and reviewed. It could be that the emphasis is on self-gratification. Self-realization leading to self-fulfillment can not be realized selfishly and this means some measure of sacrifice must be a part of it . . . an occasional act of self-control and self-deprivation in consideration of others is part and parcel of this concept. Our society submerges, along with the poor, the idea of sacrifice and pain, yet there is no pill that can eliminate either one completely. Children in their fanciful wonder-world will need to be guided out of it with the utmost care and honesty to the inevitable responsibility of maturity and the realization of the imperfections that plague man and his efforts.

Children who have an opportunity to bask in affection and under-standing, who are led through a positive life of trust and security in the early stages of their journey to fulfillment will later in life not be defeated when they encounter frustrations. These children, upon growing up can envision a "good" and safe world because they had a glimpse of it as youngsters.

It could be that each growing generation can achieve self-reliance only when surrounded by teachers who can apply, make work and adjust varying degrees of "mother-hen complexes" and varying degrees of recep-tivity to the in loco parentes concept . . . new trends not withstanding!

Truth has ever been a controversial term and concept. What is truth? Truth, said Mark Van Doren, is what the teacher is expected to be concerned with . . . What is it? Long ago Descartes said, "I think, therefore, I am." This is exactly a point of truth that teachers can accept because this is what the teacher's work entails, the encourage-ment of potential thinkers to acquire skill in the act of truly thinking.

Practically every book treating education will have pages and pages on possible aids that might help students to think reflectively, scien-tifically, creatively, purposefully, etc. So, potential thinkers do exist, teachers <u>do</u> exist, and the task of teachers is to help potential thinkers acquire skill in thinking. This is a fact that can be accepted as the truth--remembering that out of all the factors in this truth some may differ quantitatively and qualitatively.

Once one truth is established other truths will more readily follow. The next "logical axiom" appears to be that these potential thinkers will have to think <u>something</u>. What will it be? Judgments of this sort have concerned men for centuries:

> . . . For men are by no means agreed about the things to be taught, whether we aim at virtue or the best life. Neither is it clear whether education should be more concerned with intellectual or moral virtue. Existing practice is perplexing; no one knows on what principle we should proceed. Should the useful in life, or should virtue, or should higher knowledge, be the aim of our training?[16]

Robert M. Hutchins would have the classic and liberal arts emphasized:

> One purpose of education is to draw out the elements of our common human nature. These elements are the same in any time or place.[17]

By contrast John Dewey insists:

> The most direct blow at traditional separation of doing and knowing and at the traditional prestige of purely "intellectual" studies, however, has been given by the progress of experimental science. If progress has demonstrated anything, it is that there is no such thing as genuine knowledge and fruitful understanding except as the offspring of <u>doing</u>.[18]

Mortimer J. Adler is a staunch defender of "good habits".

---

[16]
Louise Ropes Loomis (ed), Aristotle on Man and Universe: Metaphysics, Parts of Animals, Ethics, Politics, Poetics. "Politics", (New York: Walter J. Black, 1943), Book VIII, Chapter 2, Paragraph 1, p. 412.

[17]
Robert M. Hutchins, The Higher Learning in America (New Haven, Conn.: Yale University Press, 1936), pp. 64-67.

[18]
John Dewey, Democracy and Education (New York: The MacMillan Company, 1916), pp. 321-322.

Clearly, then, a man is not bettered simply by habit formation, for if habits be bad they impede the development of his total nature by violating the tendency of his powers to their own perfection. In short, human nature, partly constituted by its natural potencies at birth, is bettered or perfected in the course of life only through the formation of good habits.[19]

In 1861, Herbert Spencer offered the following areas of fundamental studies which he felt were necessary to continue human life:

. . . 1. those activities which directly administer to self-preservation; 2. those activities which, by securing the necessaries of life, indirectly minister to self-preservation; 3. those activities which have for their end the rearing and discipline of offspring; 4. those activities which are involved in the maintenance of proper social and political relations; 5. those miscellaneous activities which fill up the leisure part of life, devoted to the gratification of tastes and feelings.[20]

George F. Kneller, in his book Introduction to Philosophy, quotes Pope Pius XI as follows:

According to Pope Pius XI: Education consists essentially in preparing man for what he must be and for what he must do here below in order to attain the sublime end for which he was created. . . The subject of education is man whole and entire, soul united to body in unity of nature, with all faculties natural and supernatural, such as right reason and revelation show him to be. . . [21]

How may formal and informal teaching adults, come to an agreement in the choice of subject matter content? It is difficult for adults to agree on what should be presented to the young for their thinking pleasure. Human beings eagerly accept this challenge and continuously revise their offerings, some will often appear overwhelmed: "To some

---

19
Mortimer J. Adler, "In Defense of the Philosophy of Education," National Society for the Study of Education, Forty-first Yearbook, Part I, Philosophies of Education (Chicago: University of Chicago Press, 1942), pp. 239-243.

20
Herbert Spencer, Education, Moral and Spiritual (London: G. Manwaring, 1861), pp. 7-9.

21
George F. Kneller, Introduction to Philosophy (New York: John Wiley and Sons, Inc., 1964), p. 21.

it may seem an admission of defeat to assert that it is impossible to draw our theories and practices of education out of some system of absolute truth."[22]

Systems of absolute truth can certainly be drawn from the fundamental biological, sociological and psychological needs of human beings. Human drives seem to be everywhere the same. It seems that in emphasizing individual differences, educated adults may have by-passed innate human similarities. "The basic goal for teachers is to treat pupils alike in areas where they are alike, but treat them differently in areas where they are different."[23] Children are first human beings and then they are members of an ethnic group, a nationality, a class, or a citizen of a specific century. By virtue of being human beings, all children everywhere deserve the best that any society has to offer.

History occasionally gives us a flash of appreciation concerning cause and effect. With time, and in perspective, historians can interpret the rise and fall of societies and civilizations. These interpretations often rest on the unmistakable evidence presented by the existing circumstances of education and of the teaching of the young.

Every society educates its young; the best societies seem consciously to lead their young "from capacities to abilities, from ignorances to knowledges, /and/ from impulses to ideals; /all of this in the framework of/ knowing, feeling, and doing."[24]

Recent major world events seem to point out the need for some very definite systems of absolute truth, as Brameld has asked, how else can mankind "analyze and organize the premise upon which he conducts his political, scientific, aesthetic, religious, and educational practices?" Are basic human needs the answer?

Such events as "nuclear energy, international tensions, the Soviet Union, thrusts into space, fluctuations in foreign policy, racial segregation /and desegregation/ middle-class culture, distortion of values,

---

22

Edward H. Reisner, "Philosophy and Science in the Western World: A Historical View," The Forty-First Yearbook of the National Society for the Study of Education, Part I Philosophies of Education, Edited Nelson B. Henry (Chicago: The University of Chicago Press, 1942), Chapter I, p. 37.

23

Willard C. Olson, Child Development, Second Edition, (Boston: D.C. Heath and Company, 1959), p. 275.

24

C.S.C. Cunningham, Ph.D., The Pivotal Problems of Education (New York: The Macmillan Company, 1960), pp. 5, 6, 7.

television scandals,"[25] and more recently the revelations of the Powell, Baker, Hoffa, and Dodd cases, not to mention the C.I.A. and crime disclosures, point out the need for a special kind of teaching content. Daily reading of newspapers can add a few more such "happenings" to this list. How do these events affect teachers? Manning M. Pattillo answers this question admirably:

> If our graduates are to take their proper place in the world-wide struggle for a free society, if they are to understand the meaning of their own existence, if they are to have firm guidelines for their own lives, our undergraduate colleges must give more attention to human and humane values. We must encourage each student to develop a coherent philosophy, a body of values which he has examined critically, has embraced, and can apply to the decisions of personal and public life. He cannot be "given" such a philosophy. He must work it out for himself with the encouragement of wise teachers who have expertness in the realm of values. We cannot expect this to happen fortuitously; there must be planned opportunities for the student to grapple with the deep problems of values facing mankind. It is the mark of a good teacher that he can guide the student's judgment in such an effort and still leave him free to reach his own conclusions. It is not necessary or desirable that all arrive at the same philosophy. It is urgent that all work at the problem. In a world in which humane values are gravely threatened, we cannot afford to fail in this task.[26]

A recent article, "Is Literature Dehumanizing Us," in the Christian Science Monitor indentifies literature as one source which seemingly contributes to this grave threatening of human values. The author of the article quotes Reverend J. Regan, Dean of St. John's University Colleges of Liberal Arts and Sciences, Brooklyn, New York:

> Let us not forget that, in the last analysis censorship, governmental or private, is only a defensive weapon. It does little to form the moral climate of the nation. Excessive reliance on it only weakens the cause of morality. The vigilant parent and the well formed conscience are still the strongest opponents of the purveyor of obscenity. Our chief work for the future is to encourage the reading of good literature and the patronizing of good films .....

25
   Brameld, op. cit., pp. 2-11, 21.

26
   Manning M. Pattillo, "Resolving the Conflict of Purpose Between the Search for Truth and the Teaching of Values," Current Issues in Higher Education: Higher Education Reflects on the Larger Society, G. Kerry Smith (ed.), (Washington, D.C. Association for Higher Education, 1966), p. 113.

Perhaps I can best summarize my position in the words of Fr. Murray: "Our Chief problem. . . is not literary censorship, but literary creation."[27]

Pamela Smith summarizes the article in the following manner:

The literary quotas of violence and pornography continue to increase. Few responsible individuals would advocate censorship. But more and more people, including the writers themselves, are convinced that social and moral consequences must be faced.[28]

The Spanish-speaking student caught between cultures needs more help than other students in cultivating the skill of picking the best from the old culture and the best from the new culture. Perhaps teachers of Spanish-speaking students have a special significant duty to perform in this area?

The awakening of underdeveloped countries and groups hasten a transformation of cultures at horrifying speeds. If schools and teachers lag in their catalytic work of keeping humans human and of improving this condition, the situation could develop into a crisis in which "mass-man" as described by Ortega Y Gasset, would be in charge of world affairs making the future outlook, to say the least, less than admirable:

. . . we live at a time when man believes himself capable of creation, but he does not know what to create. Lord of all things, he is not lord of himself. He feels lost amid his own abundances. . . The meaning is that the type of man dominant today is a primitive one, a _Naturmensch_ rising up in the midst of a civilized world. The world is civilized, its inhabitant is not: he does not see the civilization of the world around him, but he uses it as if it were a natural force. . . The actual mass-man is, in fact, a primitive who has slipped through the wings on to the age-old stage of civilization. . . . . The mass-man has no attention to spare for reasoning, he learns only in his own flesh. . . . . But today it is man who is the failure, because he is unable to keep pace with the progress of his own civilization. . . . The most "cultured" people today are suffering from an

---

27
    Pamela Smith, "Is Literature Dehumanizing Us?" Christian Science Monitor, Second Section (Saturday, August 5, 1967), p. 11.

28
    Ibid.

incredible ignorance of history.[29]

Dawson explains his interpretation of life today by saying:

> This is the age of Frankenstein, the hero who created a mech-
> anical monster and then found it had got out of control and
> threatened his own existence. Frankenstein represents our
> age even more truly than Faust represented the age of Goethe
> and the romantics. Western man has created the technological
> order, but has not discovered how to control it. It is
> beginning to control him, and if it does, there seems no way
> of preventing it from destroying him.[30]

Teachers, using technology courageously but judiciously, must teach
more than the scientific, technological mode of "modern life"--teachers
have the responsibility of developing in the learner a feeling based on
accurate knowledge of their great historic spirit and principles earned
by countless other human beings in the past and given to the present
learner as a hopeful gift for better living. If the gift and the givers
of the gift are ignored, the foundations upon which this civilization
rests will crumble away. "It is of great importance, then, to understand thoroughly this mass-man with his potentialities of the greatest
good and the greatest evil."[31]

The learner of today must understand and feel a sense of gratitude
(knowing that mistakes were made) for the heritage proferred him by the
labor and suffering of the world of the past. The young of times past
faced uncertainty, too, and probably were bewildered by changes occurring
then, but they "overcame". No matter how imperfectly performed (and who
is perfect?) the task of building a new nation was accomplished. Students of the moment are being charged with the same task now. They are
asked to take this trust and to make it better for the next generation.
Many thousands of students are splendidly responding. The teacher plays
an inescapably responsible role in this education of one generation for
another generation. Whenever there is an appearance of a Sunset Strip,
a "Happenings" group or a few hundred "hippies"[32] the fact is self

---

29
  Jose Ortega y Gasset, The Revolt of the Masses (New York: W.W.
Norton and Company, Inc., 1960), pp. 44, 82, 85, 91.

30
  Christopher Dawson, The Crisis of Western Education (New York:
Sheed and Ward, Inc., 1961), p. 189.

31
  Ortega y Gasset, op. cit., p. 53.

32
  Wainwright London, "The Strange New Love Land of the Hippies,"
Life (March 31, 1967), Vol. 62, No. 13, p. 15.

apparent, adults have somehow failed.

Leaders in education, teachers, must never forget that even the scientific method owes its existence to many past humble searchers for the truth and therefore they can expect that their own students who will be the scientists of tomorrow will be worthy ones: "Scientists of all kinds should become more than scientists; they should become citizens deeply concerned for the social import of their achievements..."[33]

Happily, however, the realization of how "decisions can become fateful for the very survival of our civilization"[34] has resulted in a recent formal listing of educational values which we can accept as truths:

Respect for the Worth and Dignity of Every Individual. Faith in man's ability to make Rational Decisions. . . Shared Responsibility for the Common Good, Emotional Health, Freedom to Teach and Excellence for all.[35]

For many years, now, scholars, educators, academicians, specialists, technicians, students and the whole cohort of persons interested in the teaching-learning process have been searching and researching avenues that could lead to improvement of the teaching process.

Out of this research many fine aids have been selected, many are being tried, and some have been fully accepted as "good", but caution should be exercised in the use of a few of these materials. They cannot be used exactly as the researchers used them:

All have something to say about learning, very often with reference to experiments. How are we to regard their advice? I think the fairest view is that education is very like cookery. There is some very good cooking going on and a lot that is not very good, some being well-nigh poisonous. Some day there may be a real science of cookery based on

---

33
   Brameld, op. cit., p. 180.

34
   Niebuhr Reinhold, Our Moral and Spiritual Resources for International Cooperation. U.S. National Commission for UNESCO, Citizen Consultation Series (Washington, D.C.: The Commission, 1956), p. 36.

35
   Project on the Instructional Program of the Public Schools, Education in a Changing Society, Richard I. Miller, Associate Director, Writer of this Report, Second Printing, (Washington, D.C. National Education Association, 1964), pp. 9-12.

physics, chemistry and biology but these sciences are not yet advanced enough to tell the good cook more than he has found out by rule-of-thumb, though they can often tell the bad cook what not to do. Good cooking is a matter of experience, skill, good recipes, sound materials and the right conditions. Much the same is true of good teaching.

Another important point of resemblance between cookery and teaching is that most really successful cooks stick to well-tried methods and though they may experiment occasionally they maintain a high customary level by relying on recipes which they know to be good. The same is true of the success-ful teacher. . . He may not hit the educational headlines and he is the despair of the educational reformer. . . . but he gets results and the children trust him.[36]

Adults in any country cannot safely ignore the astounding world achievements in transportation and communication. It is no longer pos-sible to theoretically, in ignorance of actuality, to pontificate con-cerning peoples. The incredibly fast means of going places, reaching and listening to people is swiftly changing many of the world's tenaciously held preconceived determining tendencies.

Only as American citizens come to discover what human beings everywhere are really like--and as citizens of other count-ries similarly come to understand Americans--can we honestly hope to weaken the blockages of mutual suspicion and falsifi-cation. . .[37]

When we "discover what human beings everywhere are really like," we will discover that they are all different in being themselves and they are alike in belonging to the human race. . . communication must be the key.

This change and trend demands that language facility be given top priority in educational programs.

Indeed, the whole picture of human achievement, marred as it so often is by folly and by malice, points to human capabil-ities unknown to other animals, to intellectual and moral capacities that cry out for the development which is education.

36
   Patrick Meredith, Learning, Remembering and Knowing (New York: Association Press, 1961), pp. 46-47.

37
   Brameld, op. cit., p. 126.

Perhaps the most obvious example is that of language.[38]

Most good living results from accurate facile language activity; therefore, one of the distinguishing marks of a master teacher is his exceptional ability to manipulate a great fund of sound knowledge concerning language and its effective use. This part of his professionalism was mentioned before.

To summarize, if schools in the United States, staffed by master teachers, are to expedite the hopes for a new society, these master teachers must effectively spearhead the fight against ignorance. Their high sophistication and strong personal commitment will demand that they seek the cooperation and help of all other adults as they strive for: (1) healthy, strong, secure, stable and moral lives of their own; (2) broad, rich, and informed professionalism; (3) constant, deep search for truth; (4) willingness to change attitudes; (5) sound knowledge of human nature, historically rooted; (6) artistry in sensitive, knowledgeable timing; (7) acceptance of the oneness of the world and all its peoples; (8) increased awareness of the dignity, responsibility, and enjoyment of teaching; (9) expectation of satisfying, exhausting, and uplifting work; and (10) a willingness to give and receive affection.

It is evident that in this technological, global everchanging and fast moving world the persons responsible for the education of its future citizens are confronted with complex choices in the selection and application of educational content, in the identification and pursuit of worthwhile goals, and in the constructive and effective use of methods, devices, and techniques.

The tools of teaching, especially the expensive "showy" mechanized ones are a prod, a thorn to most of the teaching force. The pressure to convert to automation in teaching is tremendous. This is a scientific age and automation is one of its greatest tools. If it works in agriculture, in industry, in medicine, and in the exploration of space and ocean floors it must work in education. There is no doubt but that much of the "hardware" is useful when used judiciously but all master teachers should be on the "red alert" for a runaway Frankenstein.

Amid all tensions and pressures of modern living, the main concern of master teachers remains the same--man in his dignity preserved and enhanced--the struggle in this age as in other ages for ultimate human fulfillment. Anything that tends to detract, remove or diminish this dignity from man is to be immediately and carefully deleted from the

---

38
    Herbert Johnston, A Philosophy of Education (New York: McGraw-Hill Company, Inc., 1963), pp. 31-32.

educational process repertory.

To weaken, in any way, individuals' potentials to know is a barbaric act that results in barbarism for all. To deny to the Spanish-speaking learner the opportunity to learn English quickly--the legal language of the United States--is to freeze his potential and to condemn him to a life without much dignity and honor.

Finding the answer to some of these problems is a worthwhile--and also worldwide--goal. The goal involves problems of communication, and language is a fundamental part of communication. It is time to take a comprehensive look into the matter of language teaching in the United States.

CHAPTER IV

METHODS CURRENTLY USED IN TEACHING
SPANISH-SPEAKING CHILDREN

Chapter II introduced some of the early materials and methods used
in the teaching of English to non-English-speaking students. It was
found that although they were traditional and conservative, some
teachers failed. It could be that they did so, not because of materials
and methods in use at that time, but because of their attitudes toward
the children.

Attitudes of teachers toward students, if not prejudiced, are the
sparks which light the flame of desire to learn in the minds of children.
But, the Spanish-speaking children, to so many teachers, were aliens and
foreigners and not capable of learning. These teachers failed and, because of them the children failed.

> Contempt for the alien is not the only possible solution of
> our present contact with races and nationalities. It is
> not even a scientifically founded solution. Traditional
> Anglo-Saxon intolerance is a local and temporal cultural-
> trait like any other. Even people as nearly of the same
> blood and culture as the Spanish have not had it, and race
> prejudice in the Spanish-settled countries is a thoroughly
> different thing from that in countries dominated by England
> and the United States. . . . .
> . . . The recognition of the cultural basis of race prejudice
> is a desperate need in present world civilization.[1]

Explosively, world conditions seem to have reached a point where
cooperation must supersede competition and where intolerance can have
no place.[2] Yet, the situation daily accumulates concentrated subpoints
of disastrous danger areas because peoples of the earth cannot understand

---

[1]
Ruth Benedict, Patterns of Culture, 18th Printing, with an Introduction by Franz Boas and A New Preface by Margaret Mead (New York:
The New American Library of World Literature, Inc., a Mentor Book, 1960),
pp. 24-25.

[2]
Melvin S. Brooks, The Social Problems of Migrant Farm Laborers
(Carbondale, Illinois: Southern Illinois University, Department of
Sociology, 1960). Monograph; David Caplonity, The Poor Pay More (New
York: Free Press of Glenroe, 1963); James Bryant Conant, Slums and Sub-
urbs (New York: McGraw-Hill Book Company, 1961), pp. 1-144; Ralph L.
Pounds, James R. Bryner, The School in American Society, Second Edition
(New York: The MacMillan Company, 1967), pp. 1-457.

one another well enough to discuss the issues which concern them all.

Communication avenues are many. The technological advances in this area are almost beyond belief, but _understanding_ is still lacking.

It is this author's opinion that no longer can leaders of the United States say unequivocably that this nation is predominantly English-speaking, Protestant, Anglo, White and Middle-class. There are too many citizens who do not fit this pattern to make the phrase either believable or applicable. These masses of people are stirring, beginning to move, demanding that their needs be met. It behooves all citizens and most especially teachers to pay heed to the "rumblings" of this potential giant.[3]

The poor have similar educational problems wherever found. The degree of severity and the quality of causes may differ; the ratio of numbers of people and problems can vary, but the problems strangely seem related and much the same. So, what is said of New York City's _poor_ could very well be true of Alamosa's poor.

> Evidence that the public school favors the affluent and works to the detriment of the poor continues to accumulate. Intel-lectual advances made last summer by Head Start pre-schoolers were soon dissipated in the traditional kindergartens in New York City--those pupils are a minimum of two years behind in reading, with twice that number by the eighth grade--are from racial ghettos and poor neighborhoods; and we have known for some time that in a Harlem ghetto school a youngster's I.Q. drops the longer he remains in grade school. . . . . The integration of eight totally segregated black and white schools in New York City under the Princeton plan of pairing schools, for example, showed that the negro poor profited educationally; but it also showed that the middle-class

---

3
   Bernard Asbell, "A Surprising Report on Our Worst School: Not Like Other Children," Red Book, Vol. 121, No. 6 (October, 1963), pp. 64-114, 120; Walter Fogel, "Education and Income of Mexican-Americans in the Southwest," Mexican-American Study Report (Los Angeles, California: Division of Research Graduate School of Business Administration, University of California, 1965), Advance Report I; Barbara H. Kemp, The Youth We Haven't Served: A Challenge to Vocational Education (Washington, D.C.: U.S. Office Government Printing Office, 1966), p. 46; Alice Ogle, "Gallegos and Some Spanish-Speaking Realities," Ave Maria, Vol. 101, No. 5 (January 31, 1965), pp. 10-13; Henry Santistevan, ed., "Viva La Causa! The Rising Expectations of the Mexican-American," IUD Agenda Vol. 2, No. 7 (July, 1966), pp. 1-20; Louisa R. Shotwell, "What Kind of Harvest?" Presbyterian Life, Vol. 14, No. 13 (July 1, 1961), pp. 15-19, 32; Joseph Wilson, Appalachia; Special Ave Report," Ave Maria (March, 1966), pp. 6-11.

students profited twice as much.[4]

The revealing word in the above quote is the word <u>poor</u>. The throwing of these students together under the carefully reconstructed teaching situations and the exposing of the students to excellent teachers and materials plus the actual face to face meeting of each other would certainly produce improvement of education because <u>attitudes</u> changed.

Ruth Benedict in her book <u>Patterns</u> <u>of</u> <u>Culture</u> said, "Since we are forced to believe that the race of man is one species, it follows that man everywhere has an equally long history behind him."[5] It is the shameful neglect of the recognition of each one's "long history" that causes most educational problems. This is the reason the giant mentioned before is starting to move, here in the United States and everywhere in the world. Ruth Benedict continues:

> Social thinking at the present time has no more important task before it than that of taking adequate account of cultural relativity. In the fields of both sociology and psychology the implications are fundamental, and modern thought about contacts of peoples and about our changing standards is greatly in need of sane and scientific direction.[6]

There are many important well documented facts concerning people; our knowledge of students and of learning has broadened with extraordinary speed, but these facts and knowledges are not particularly well known by the majority of adults.

> There is no longer any serious doubt about potential equality or near-equality of the so-called races, nor is there any doubt whatever that variability among peoples is greater <u>within</u> groups than it is between groups. This fact must be known.[7]

4
Maurice R. Berube, "The Urban School: Education and the Poor," The Commonweal, Vol. LXXXVI, No. 2 (March 31, 1967), p. 46.

5
Benedict, op. cit., p. 30.

6
Ibid., p. 239.

7
Floyd L. Ruch, Psychology and Life, Sixth Edition, (Chicago: Scott, Foresman and Company, 1963), p. 489.

It seems wise to be aware of other people's feelings of "self". This is another area of knowledge that is perhaps known but not acted upon. "It often galls the Spanish-speaking citizen to have some well-meaning individual say, 'all you have to do to succeed is to be more like an Anglo'.[8]

Each person has an implicit need to be himself and none other. This implies that in certain instances and conditions each person needs to behave like others, but always with his own stamp of selfhood.

Language usage by the time a child enters school is very much a part of selfhood. How criminal it is that when a Spanish-speaking child comes to school he is commanded not to speak Spanish but to speak English...his 30,000 words or less of oral vocabulary are not useful because the teacher is ignorant of the fact that they exist.

How flagrantly this violates the psychological teaching principle of "take the child from where he is to where you want him to be!" No teacher can tell where a child should be until he knows where he has been. This is the kind of teacher, administrator, and community attitude that needs to be changed so that the stirring giant may be constructively brought to life. All adults need to know where every child is and what made him what he is so that they may better serve him.

In teaching English to non-English-speaking children the realization that the children are not devoid of all knowledge just because they cannot express themselves in English is a sound generalization. Teachers should be required to take at least one language[9] other than English (if they are English-speaking) in order to experience some of the frustrations that accompany such an undertaking. Thus, they can have a faint idea of how it feels to be in a position where there is very little mutual understanding. They can, then, develop a better feeling for the Spanish-speaking child or any other child, who is in the process of learning English for the first time.

Three methods currently being used individually or in combination are: (1) Teaching English as a Second Language, (2) Teaching English as a Foreign Language, and (3) Teaching English as a Foreign Language

---

[8]
Ogle, op. cit., p. 12.

[9]
Maria Urquides, Aqui Se Habla Espanol and English: Tucson's Tale of Two Cultures, NEA Journal, Vol. 56, No. 2 (February, 1967), pp. 62, 82-89.

Which Must Become a Primary Language.

First Method

In the United States, Teaching English as a Second Language has not been too successful (refer to Chapter II). This kind of teaching can only result and generally did result in superficially teaching just enough English for the student to muddle unmeaningfully through, in a retarded, substandard manner, to the third, fourth, fifth, or even the sixth grade. The teachers were not able to motivate the students and the students felt no urgent need to be motivated.

It took many years to sap the pride and initiative of these people;--no ability to speak English and so no job--no job, no money to go to school and learn English--it will take a correspondingly long time to remedy this sad state of affairs. Patience and understanding will be needed by all concerned and a determined, long-term, organized, consistent effort must be maintained. Above all, a vision of what can be must fill the minds of the teachers and the taught.

In the Southwest, Spanish, in most instances, remained the primary language although formal growth and development of it vanished as soon as the student began to attend the schools of his country. Thus, the student became limited in the use of both languages. In attitudes, habits, skills, appreciations, and facts he progressed almost entirely within the Spanish culture ethos. Because his reading ability was limited in English and almost non-existent in Spanish, he did not learn about his rights as a citizen of the United States but he also did not learn about the great heritage bequeathed to him by his forefathers.

If this student, multiplied many times, is now and has been for some generations on welfare or on worse than slavery conditions (migrants), the schools of this country should bear some responsibility for the situation and should immediately start a thoughtful reconstruction of educational action toward a transformation of what exists.

Many attempts of find teachers to teach English As a Second Language,[10] in fact, resulted in the teaching of English as a Foreign

---

[10] Faye Bumpass, Teaching Young Students English as a Second Language (Chicago: American Book Company, 1963). Miss Bumpass has a Series of Booklets for Beginners; Mary Finocchiaro, Teaching English as a Second Language (San Francisco: Henry Holt and Company, 1963), pp. 1-400; Afton Dill Nance, Teaching English as a Second Language to Elementary School Pupils, Report of Education Study Group, Third Annual Conference on Families who Follow the Crops (Sacramento, California: California

Language. Numerous English-speaking teachers and Spanish-speaking teachers have been master teachers in the past and have actually done more than help students "muddle through".

The success which these teachers experienced was mainly due to their sensitive appreciation of the value systems involved. This appreciation armed them with attitudes which opened up the communication channel. The writer of this paper is grateful to teachers of this calibre. Dedicated master teachers are constantly working to improve the teaching-learning situation at all levels and in many places:

> At Lincoln Elementary School in La Junta, where approximately 90% of the pupils are Spanish and bilingual (?), an ungraded primary unit has been successfully operating for the last three years. . . Not including the kindergarten, there are 14 groups in the primary unit, six in the first with three first grade teachers, four in the second with two teachers, and four in the third with one teacher. Children are promoted from group to group, but do not repeat...[11]

Dr. Wilder Penfield, former Director of the Montreal Neurological

---

State Department of Education, 1962); Mamie Sizemore, Bibliography for Teachers of English as a Second Language (Phoenix 7, Arizona: State Department of Education, Division of Indian Education, 1960). Nine pages of 92 items of very fine occasionally annotated references from 1947 to 1960. Five bibliographies listed; Hubert A. Coleman, "The Relationship of Socio-Economic Status to the Performance of Junior High School Students," Journal of Experimental Education, Volume 9 (September, 1940), pp. 61-63; William H. Burton, "Education and Social Class in the United States," Harvard Educational Review, Volume 23, No. 4 (Fall, 1953), p. 250; Otto Klineberg, "Life is Fun in a Smiling Fairskinned World," The Saturday Review, Volume XLVI, No. 7 (February 16, 1963), pp. 75-87; Education and the Disadvantaged American: Educational Policies Commission (Washington, D.C.: National Education Association, 1962), pp. 12-13; Eva White, "The Inter-Racial School--A Challenge," The Delta Kappa Gamma Bulletin, Volume XXI, No. 3 (Spring, 1955), pp. 34-42; Ben H. Bagdikian, "The Invisible Americans," The Saturday Evening Post, Volume 236, No. 45 (December 21-28, 1963), pp. 27-38; Robert J. Havighurst, Public Schools of Chicago (Chicago: The Board of Education, 1964), p.60; Margaret Anderson, "After Integration--Higher Horizons," Time Magazine, Volume CXII, No. 38, 488 (April 21, 1963), p. 10; Bruno Bettelheim, "The Decision to Fail," The School Review, Volume 69, No. 4 (Winter, 1961), pp. 377-412.

[11]
    Annotations from Department of Education, State of Colorado. Volume V, No. 7 (March, 1957), p. 7.

Institute and former Chairman of the Department of Neurology and Neuro-surgery of the McGill University wrote, "Language, when it is learned by the normal physiological process, is not taught at all."[12] This approach can be used in schools if the master teacher has the needed technical proficiency needed in the language arts and the reading fields, plus the necessary attitudes to provide as "normal a physiological" provoking climate as possible.

In Colorado, Dr. Roy McCanne studied three approaches to the teaching of reading:

(1) Teaching Spanish-speaking children using the Basal Reading Approach, the Betts Basal Reader Series, third edition by Emmett A. Betts and Carolyn M. Welch was used; (2) Teaching English As a Second Language was the next approach - Fay Bumpass - We Learn English Series and the Aural-Oral method prevailed here; (3) the last technique was The Language Experience Approach-Learning to Read Through Experience by Dorris M. Lee and R.V. Allen was the text used. The result indicated that the basal reader approach was equal to or better than the other two on 9 out of 10 hypotheses.[13]

This study tends to emphasize the need for order, organization, and definite goals in teaching. A good basal series serves as a map to reach a destination; the teacher is free to take as many detours and side trips desired, but the map gets the job done well. Dr. McCanne's study has an excellent appendix of instructional materials and the Skill Book sample.[14]

In addition to the texts mentioned in the McCanne study, there are some other sound series that have been found to help the teaching of Spanish-speaking children--Language Arts with special emphasis on Reading Skills--the writer will mention only one more, Reading for Meaning

---

[12] Penfield Wilder and Lamar Roberts, Speech and Brain Mechanisms (Princeton, New Jersey: Princeton University Press, 1959), p. 257.

[13] Roy McCanne, Study of Approaches to First Grade English Reading Instruction for Children from Spanish-Speaking Homes. Cooperative Research Project No. 2734 (Denver, Colorado: Colorado State Department of Education, 1966), pp. 1-232.

[14] Ibid., pp. 194-232.

<u>Series--Bright Peaks</u> by Paul McKee et al.[15] Available with this series is a special spiral-backed book, <u>Introducing English: An Oral Pre-Reading Program for Spanish-Speaking Primary Pupils</u> by Louise Lancaster. (See bibliography for additional recent texts in Reading and Language Arts.)

Second Method

<u>Teaching English as a Foreign Language</u> probably has been used by many teachers for many years, but has been called Teaching the Bilingual, Teaching the Spanish-Speaking[16] or has not been called by any particular title, it just happened.

The Second Method of Teaching the Spanish-speaking gained attention, support, and impetus when the FLES programs came into existence. <u>These Foreign Languages in the Elementary Schools</u>[17] programs uncovered failure in much of the foreign language teaching found in schools throughout the

---

[15]
Paul McKee, Annie McCowen, M. Lucille Harrison, Elizabeth Lehr, and William K. Durr, Reading for Meaning Series, Fourth Edition <u>Bright Peaks</u> (Boston: Houghton Mifflin Company, 1966), Whole Series.

[16]
E. Roby Leighton (Coordinator), Workshop For Teachers of Bilingual Students (Tucson, Arizona: University of Arizona Press, 1961), pp. 1-115; Theodore Huebener and Mary Finocchiaro, English for Spanish-Speaking Americans (New York: Henry Holt and Company, 1950,) pp. 1-426.

[17]
Theodore Andersson, The Teaching of Foreign Languages in the Elementary School (Boston: D.C. Heath and Company, 1953), pp. 1-119; Carlos Rivera, "The Teaching of Spanish in the First Grades of El Paso Public Schools," Hispania, Vol. 35, No. 4 (November, 1952), pp. 452-457; Margit McRae, Teaching Spanish in the Grades (Boston: Houghton Mifflin Company, 1957), pp. 1-308; C.C. Fries, Teaching and Learning English as a Foreign Language (Ann Arbor: The University of Michigan Press, 1945), pp. 1-50; W.R. Parker, The National Interest and Foreign Languages, Revised Edition, U.S. Department of State, National Commission for UNESCO, Publication 6389 (Washington, D.C., Government Printing Office, January, 1964), pp. 8-344; Ruben Lopez, "Language Laboratory," Audio-Visual News: Arizona Association for Audio-Visual Education, Volume I, No. 4 (March 20, 1962), p. 4; Paul C. McRill, "The New Foreign-Language Program and How To Tell it From the Old One," The Colorado School Journal, Volume 79, No. 5 (January, 1964), pp. 18, 19-22.

United States. In the first place, teachers teaching the foreign language, so often, did not have a sound knowledge of the language themselves. Most teachers relied on ponies and dictionaries for translations; verb declensions, grammar rules, and vocabulary memorization for class work, all of this with very little meaning or functional use. Students muddled through one, two, three or even four years of this kind of teaching. The result was that individuals involved in this kind of teaching became very skeptical of the value or status desirability of foreign language classes.

Thus, it can be said that teaching English to the Spanish-speaking and teaching a foreign language to English-speaking have related factors; the teacher, the time element, the need, the joy of accomplishment or the anxiety and frustration of failure. A language becomes identifiable and intelligible by hearing it, saying it, reading it, and writing it. Teaching English as a foreign language emphasizes the learning significance of hearing and saying (i.e.) oral-aural, audio-lingual, direct or mother-tongue approaches.[18]

It can be assumed, not safely but hopefully, that master teachers with vision and an understanding of attitudes are teaching today; that previous experience in teaching English to non-English-speaking students have taught them what to do, how to do it better, and why it needs to be done.

Third Method

The motivating, sustaining, and aspiring goal in this type of approach is to help the Spanish-speaking student become a first-class citizen. To facilitate the achievement of this goal both English and Spanish must be used. The two languages work together in harmony but with the intent of transfer from Spanish to English as rapidly as it can meaningfully happen. The two languages will change position in the student's use of them. Spanish will become a secondary language and English will become the primary one. Eventually, if the student chooses

---

[18]
Helen Harter, English is Fun or Rhythm and Song Approach to the Teaching of English to Non-English-Speaking Beginners, Second Edition (Tempe, Arizona: Helen Harter, 1962), pp. 1-82; Las Cruces Schools, Program for Non-English Speaking Beginners, Revised (Las Cruces, New Mexico: Las Cruces Schools, 1963), pp. 1-34; Mrs. Theresa Carrell, V.J. Kennedy (Staff), Preschool Instructional Program for Non-English Speaking Children, Foreword J.W. Edgar, Commissioner of Education, Texas Agency (April, 1960), pp. last few pages, excellent basic vocabulary and bibliography.

and if the schools teach languages in the elementary schools, the student could become a true bilingual, fluent in both Spanish and English.

The reason for attempting to make English the primary language is the necessity for it in order to succeed in the schools of this country and in order to succeed as an informed, participating, and responsible citizen. Spanish must be kept because it is the anchoring element which keeps the Spanish-speaking student proud and secure. It is a deep part of his consciousness of self.

Ideally, the teacher should be fluent in both languages. In any case the teacher helping students to learn English must have enough knowledge of the Spanish language and culture to constructively guide the Spanish-speaking student into the "have" group. Through the teaching of these children and through the on-purpose learning of the teacher, a communication bridge can be established quite quickly. If the teacher is going to make this kind of teaching his life's work, more information about this culture and language will be beneficial. The teacher can not help growing into a more human and humane person.

It is important that the teacher be accepted by the students and the students by the teacher. Tolerance has no place in a classroom. Who wants to be tolerated? In order to be accepted, sound knowledge is needed and genuine affection abound--virtues, faults, errors, achievements, strengths, and weaknesses recognized--in an atmosphere of mutual involvement in learning.

Straight-jacket ideas such as blind faith in I.Q. scores[19] should be discarded. Experimental research has given teachers much that is excellent but there could be biased or cloudy research also.[20] Teachers need to have more confidence in their own years of experience in the field of teaching. The "quickie" way of gaining information by surveys, questionnaires, checklists, analyses, and polls may not be the best or most reliable source all the time.

Teaching every child as a potentially gifted child is an excellent first approach. There is no need to let the cumulative report files or gossip make up the mind of the teacher. After the teacher becomes personally acquainted with the student and certain inherited and acquired qualities are revealed, the teacher may take other steps for helpful action.

---

[19]
Paul Friggens, "Is the Negro Equal in Intelligence and Ability?" Condensed from the PTA Magazine, Readers Digest, (March 20, 1964), pp. 83-87.

[20]
Martin Mayer, The Schools (New York: Harper and Brothers, 1961), pp. 108 and 376.

When the teacher is Spanish-speaking, the danger will be too much reliance on Spanish or too strong a rejection of all that is Spanish. At all times the youngsters must sense the adventurous daring of their opportunity to keep Spanish and the survival nature of the tool called English. The two languages will help them to serve their country in a special way.

At no time should a child be punished because he slips back to what he knows so well, the Spanish language. A gentle insistence on the use of English should always be in effect, the English word calmly supplied as normal procedure. As soon as the student has acquired most of the basic vocabulary words in English, the supportive attitude of the teacher can become more demanding. Parent and sibling cooperation is helpful; it should be sought.

If the two languages are part of the school system's curriculum, the mutual skill and lack of skill in each others language should help students to realize their common situation. Each group knows a language, but does not and must learn another. The English student has rarely been in this position. He could grow greatly in the understanding of the language problems of the Spanish-speaking student. Members of both of these groups will have occasional clearcut feelings of superiority and inferiority yet under the guidance of an excellent teacher all members could end their school life with a wealth of attitudes that could make a better world.

Utilizing both languages helps keep communication channels free from obstructions caused by fear and distrust. This action opens up a feeling of commonality that draws people together. When students feel this common bond, the teacher can most effectively use his accumulated knowledge of _all_ methods and techniques.

As was mentioned before, until a certain threshold of confidence is achieved, one language must be primary and the other or others secondary. This is important in order to maintain sound mental health and stability of personality. In the school life of the student, at the present time, English seems to be the language in the primary position.

To be glibly able to manipulate the English language is not the first consideration in teaching the Spanish-speaking student because ability to say words does not necessarily mean that feeling and meaning is present. It is of the utmost importance that meaning and origin of meaning be sought. Formal phonics should be carefully controlled. The conceptual increase in every subject is the crux of the matter, nothing should be left to chance. The teacher, through skillful questioning can discover misconceptions and correct them. This student can obtain, so easily, the wrong information, the wrong slant of meaning, all because he lacks experience and verbal facility in a new culture. The filling in process of ever widening meaningful concepts is the exciting challenge for teachers.

The goal is so to teach that the result will be an educated United Statesian. Being able to speak English does not preclude problems. Holding a well-paying high status job does not complete the man either. What is needed today is a man who realistically understands himself and his place in his country and the world. One who knows that he is able to help the cause of humanity anywhere.

To the Spanish-speaking, the English language is the vehicle--especially to the individual who feels alien and different--strong enough to pierce the barrier of established isolation experienced by him. Through this opening his capabilities will be released. He must know that he possesses these unique capabilities and that he can release them.

As soon as the child crosses the threshold of the classroom, he belongs! Every word, action, and thought should radiate this aura. What he knows is as important for his country's good as what others know. His language, his culture, and his home background, contribute to his nation's future greatness in proportion to his awareness of their impact on the whole. Good or bad, these influences will affect the people of the United States for a long time to come. English usage should be the force that will open the door to Spanish as well as other languages.

Because the Spanish-speaking student learns in the same way other students do, there is no need to detail methods, procedures and aids in teaching them English. This has already been done as the evidence produced by the references given proves.

Many new ideas and techniques are being advanced every day. Some of these plans claim fantastic successes as though the mellifluous era had arrived.[21]

21

    Cynthia Dee Buchanan, Teacher's Guide to Programmed Reading: Series One and Two. Sullivan Associates (New York: Webster Division, McGraw-Hill Book Company, 1964), p. 2; John Downing and Ivan Rose, "The Value of ITA: We are Enthusiastic," and Warren G. Cutts, "It's Too Soon to Know Definitely," NEA Journal, Volume 53, No. 6 (September, 1964), pp. 20, 21, 22; Foreign Language Series, Instructo Flannel Board Foreign Language Series (Philadelphia 31, Pa.: Instructo Products Co., 1962), Six complete Units; Caleb Gattegno, Background and Principles: Words in Color (Chicago: Learning Materials, Inc., a subsidiary of Encyclopaedia Britannica, Inc., 1964), Whole Series.--The author saw Dr. Gattegno demonstrate his materials and has herself used some of the charts; Jerry Johnson, Photo Phonics Language Arts Program (Flossman, Illinois: Gifted Teachers Books, Inc., 1960), Book I-II and III; Julie Hay, Mary C. Hletko and Charles E. Wingo, Reading With Phonics, Revised Edition (Philadelphia: Lippincott, 1960), Series; Ann Hughes, Carl B.

The revival of the Montessori System is being considered very carefully throughout the United States. It is already being used in some private schools in California, Denver, and in the East. The difficulty being encountered is the lack of trained personnel. At the moment the system seems to offer more strengths than weaknesses to the program of teaching the Spanish-speaking child. Montessori cannot be ignored and therefore its values should be studied and if possible used.[22]

Schools and all school personnel have not emphasized, demonstrated or demanded top-notch citizenship behavior. Psychology tells us that each generation learns all that it will know; to learn means to be taught; left untaught each generation will destroy what exists because they cannot appreciate what is there.

> Teaching is not a process of assisting wings to grow on a man, but the process of making and attaching them. Teaching is from without. Leave man lessonless and even what is of instinct in him will deteriorate. Then he retreats backward in the direction of savagery, pulling his environment back with him. Civilizing is not a job done once and for all.

Smith and Nellie Thomas, Language Arts: Beginning Reading for Disadvantaged Children. Hegler Project. Open Court Basic Series (La Salle, Illinois: Open Court Publishing Company, 1964, 1965), Monograph; Albert Mazurkiewicz, New ITA Book Early To Read Series (New York: Initial Teaching Alphabet Publications, Inc., 1964, Series.--This method is being used at Central School, Alamosa, Colorado; Glenn Mc Cracken, Charles C. Wolcutt, Mary Bond and Esther Faircloth, Basic Reading Preprimer 1-1 and Workbook 1-1, Illustrated by Carol Kitzmiller and George Wilde. (New York: J.B. Lippincott Company, 1963), p. 139; Ralph F. Robinett, A Linguistic Approach to Beginning Reading for Bilingual Children (Boston: D.C. Heath and Company, 1965), Whole Miami Series: Miss Schoolfield and Miss Timberlake, The Phonovisual Method (Washington 16, D.C. Phonovisual Products, Inc., 1959), Monograph. The author visited Primary Day Schook, 7300 River Road, Bethesada 14, Maryland, and saw the method in operation.

22
    Evelyn Beyer, "Montessori in the Space Age?" NEA Journal Volume 52, No. 9 (December, 1963), pp. 36-38; Terry Denny, "Montessori Resurrected: Now What?" Educational Forum, Volume 29, No. 6 (May, 1965), pp. 436-441; Bruce Miller, Jr., "Montessori the Model for Pre-School Education?" Grade Teacher, Volume 82, No. 7 (March, 1965), pp. 36-39, 112-117; Maria Montessori, The Montessori Method (New York: Frederick A. Stokes Co., 1919), Entire Book; Phyllis Nibling, "Montessori: Learning to Learn," Contemporary: The Sunday Denver Post (February 6, 1966), pp. 18-21; Celia Stender, "The Montessori Method," Educational Forum, Volume 29, No. 4 (May, 1965), pp. 431-435.

It is a progressive effort, not only to advance but to save itself from retrogression.[23]

The content core stressed in the third method (a combination of all that is best) is citizenship, everything else stems from this--arithmetic, science, spelling, history, all subjects will be approached from this point-of-view. The teacher will have to recognize in himself the attitudes he desires to establish in his students. He will have to develop interests and provide opportunities to reveal to the students the value system he wishes them to acquire. The transfer is not too difficult, if the teacher is aware or becomes aware of the student's existing values. This takes sensitive sincere investigation in a climate of respect. The teacher should never pre-judge or condemn, he should accept, understand and upgrade that which exists.

Teachers might have to review their own knowledge of the tools, beliefs, and channels which a government like the United States offers the teacher in order to instill in the minds of the child the value system which has made the United States the nation it is.

Some relativists might say that indoctrination is being discussed at this point. If it is, it is the kind of indoctrination that all honest people indulge in and perpetuate:

> . . . may I briefly remark here that "indoctrination" in the original sense of systematic transmission of believed values from one generation to the next, is a vice only when preventing the free personal development of the learner. Actually, it is carried on in every self-relying culture. . .[24]

Mr. Robert Ulich describes the United States as "our present wishy-washy society."[25] This country has been too permissive.

All students need to strengthen their knowledge of the powerful ideologies that have formed the base of this, the leading country in the world. Spanish-speaking students more than others need to understand--the strengths, first and the weaknesses later when they are strong themselves--that if there are shocking failures at times, it is

---

[23]
Francis Clement Kelly, Blood Drenched Altars: American Study and Comment, documentation with notes by Eber Cole Byam (Milwaukee: The Bruce Publishing Company, 1935), p. 368.

[24]
Brameld, op. cit., Foreword by Robert Ulich, p. IX.

[25]
Ibid., p. IX.

often because men fail, not ideologies.

Memorization of content has long been out-of-date in educational circles, even the term is distasteful; the new term is overlearn. But, students need to know and overlearn where this country has been and how it arrived at this present state. A state which they can physically experience but which is much harder to experience mentally, emotionally, socially, and ethically.

Suggested materials of this sort appear in the following footnote.[26]

The time has come to solidify the findings of educational research; more technical and materialistic research in the area of the teaching of human beings could continue at a slower pace. Concentrated effort is needed in change of attitudes of school personnel so that which research has already given will be fruitfully used. Books, texts, audio-visual aids, experimental resources, reinforcing techniques, etc., are not very effective by themselves. The teachers must accept the responsibility which is theirs.

Knowledgeable teachers of teachers with practice in teaching as well as in theory can surround prospective teachers with all the necessary aids in every known field of teaching-learning. Libraries and communication media centers are invaluable sources of help. During the internship experience, prospective teachers should be oriented and strengthened in this incredibly satisfying work of helping the uninformed to inform themselves.

As was mentioned before, it was not the intention of the author to, in detail, repeat, rehash, or relist examples of contents, methods, theories, aims, etc. Splendid references are now easily accessible. From these available sources the wise teacher may select and collect his own materials and adjust them to his own use.

The following recommendations to master teachers might facilitate

---

26
Gordon McClosky, et al, Introduction to Teaching in American Schools (New York: Harcourt, Brace and Company, Inc., 1954), Appendix, pp. 449-451.
Declaration of Independence, 1776.
Bill of Rights (United States Constitution), 1791
From Declaration of the Rights of Man, France, 1789
Universal Declaration of Human Rights United Nations, 1948
From the Constitution of the United Nations. Educational, Scientific and Cultural Organization, 1946
Code of Ethics, National Education Association of the United States, 1952 of (Revised)
Ralph L. Pounds and James R. Bryner, op. cit., pp. 457-460.
The Nature of Democratic Values and Processes--

their efforts in guiding the Spanish-speaking students from one culture to the other. The paramount intent being to keep the best from one culture and to select the best from the other.

Recommendations

1. Use efficiently what research and experience have already provided.

2. Realistically teach the young for a future which will bring advantages and disadvantages...teach them honesty, courage, and fortitude along with academic excellence.

3. Change the content of books now in use, the day of TV and science fiction living is not here for the masses of people. They need to start with what they know and have experienced. To do this parents are needed.

4. Encourage everyone to review the past history of man (United Statesian) noticing the accomplishments first and as maturity increases study the errors. Past history will teach us well if we withhold judgment and eliminate sentimentality.

5. Bring alive the oneness of people everywhere, not denying differences or weaknesses or strengths, but accepting common goals, hopes, and aspirations with the full realization of the results of alternative behavior.

6. Gratefully enjoy and demonstrate the dignity enhancing findings of science, accepting the responsibility for future generations. Experiment carefully in making humans more human.

7. Accept the challenge of the value of affection in opposition to hate. Arouse students to the concept of service. If governments fail, it is because man fails.

8. Develop materials emphasizing the selected content necessary to achieve survival.

9. Involve parents in this kind of education. It would be better to teach parents along with the Head Start children than to try to teach the children alone. Parents need to change their attitudes, also.

10. Make the spirit of change a positive adventure. Great dangers and great opportunities have always existed. Every generation meets its own. This generation is a competent one and it can successfully meet its own.

Dr. Bonner, a prominent scientist, recently commented, "the inevitable culmination /of the growth7 of the two cultures /of haves and have nots7 are poor because they have missed the opportunity to learn the tool (English) that would help them join the ranks of the <u>haves</u>."[27] It is urgent that teachers redouble their efforts to quickly and constructively teach English to the Spanish-speaking students.

---

[27]
    Robert C. Cowen, "The Prosperity Gap is Widening," Christian Science Monitor, Second Section (April 10, 1967, Monday), p. 9.

CHAPTER V

ALAMOSA, COLORADO, IN THE SAN LUIS VALLEY

Times have changed, the antagonistic feeling between the two culture groups is fading. Occasionally there are minor flareups, usually caused by some stranger coming into the San Luis Valley and making ignorant statements. Sometimes, old feuds and religious misunderstandings are inadvertently stirred up (i.e.) cattleman vs. sheepman, Penitente Rites, and old Spanish Land Grants.

The two groups meet together well at high income levels, although the social intermingling is still not high. The poor are still across the tracks and the streets are unpaved. This condition is rapidly changing with the introduction of a new low-income housing project provided by some federal funds. These streets are paved but not too many parents with children live there.

The following list designates the per cent of total white, Spanish surname population (1960 census), county by county, in the San Luis Valley.[1]

County	Per Cent	Total Population
Alamosa	24.9	2,494
Conejos	53.1	4,476
Costilla	72.6	3,065
Mineral	0.7	3
Rio Grande	31.2	3,477
Saguache	31.5	1,411

Teacher attitudes are, for the most part, better. In Alamosa, excellent, well-qualified Spanish-speaking origin teachers are doing a magnificent job in proving to one and all that they _can_ be professional and responsible members of the teaching family. These teachers daily present to the students an example of what can be; they are available for counseling and for informal guidance; they can act as interpreters on occasion; they can draw the attention of the other teachers to matters of cultural differences; there might be a time when the Spanish-speaking origin teacher's presence in the school could be the students' protection against rampant prejudice.

At the present time there are fourteen Spanish-speaking origin

---

[1]
  Herschel T. Manual, Spanish-Speaking Children of the Southwest: Their Education and the Public Welfare (Austin, Texas: University of Texas Press, 1965), pp. 199, 200-207.

teachers employed in the RE-11J System.[2] This number is not 29.-30.0 per cent of the total number of teachers. One reason for this is that a qualified teacher with this kind of background can find better paying jobs in larger cities and in other states. Pero, d Quien sabe? Perhaps more teachers would stay in Alamosa if more were hired. There are more unprofessional people hired than professional as the ten cooks and ten custodians[3] working in the system prove. Yet, this is a good record in the San Luis Valley where there are a few schools that subtly refrain from hiring Spanish-speaking-origin teachers in their systems.

The Head Start program is in effect in Alamosa, but some of the very poor children are not being reached. The great value in this activity is the home visitation aspect of it and the parent involvement in it. The children gain somewhat, but they lose, also. Home is a much better place for them at this age. The mothers and fathers need aid and knowhow in providing for their children what the Head Start program attempts to do. The family unit could be seriously disrupted by this program and the mental health of the children and parents could be impaired. Young children placed in a wholesome, well provided atmosphere for part of the day and then sent home to an atmosphere of want and inarticulate fear can become confused and insecure.

In Alamosa, there are three primary elementary schools; East Alamosa, Boyd, and Central. Kindergartens are now provided in each of these schools. An upper grades elementary school serves the three primary schools as does one junior high school. A new high school was recently built west and north of town. One of the new facilities gained by this action was cafeteria service. There are buses provided, but somehow there are poor children who must walk to and from school.

The approximate enrollment of the Spanish surname students enrolled in the first grades of the three primary schools for the past five years was found to be as follows:[4]

School	Principal		Per Cent
East Alamosa	Mr. Isaac Ortega		3.0
Boyd	Mr. Isaac Ortega		48. - 50.0
Central	Mr. Gary Stephens		16.0
		Average	29. - 30.0

---

[2] Personal interview with Dr. Joseph Weber, Superintendent, School District RE-11J, April 26, 1967.

[3] Ibid.

[4] Personal interview with Mr. Isaac Ortega, East Alamosa and Boyd Schools Principal, April 24, 1967.

Mr. Ortega stated that many families have left Alamosa in search for better jobs; most of the parents who have remained in Alamosa are permanent residents, not more than one per cent could be classed as transient. Not all of the children can be termed poor, but too many can. Mr. Ortega laughed as he mentioned the fact that more and more coyotes[5] are registering in the schools. Coyotes is a term used by the Spanish-speaking people to designate children of mixed parentage, in this case "English" and "Spanish." There are many children with English sounding names who are culturally Spanish. These children are not counted in the Spanish surname category.

At the high school level, the following figures were available:[6]

Year	Spanish-Speaking Surname	Total Student Graduating
1959	25	97
1960	39	108
1961	24	111
1962	24	114
1963	30	129
1964	39	120
1965	49	166
1966	38	150
1967	49	154*

*16 dropouts out of 31.

"Twenty-five to twenty-six per cent of all graduates are Spanish-speaking," said Mr. Sam Lincoln. "More, many more show potential, but drop out before the day of graduation," he added. Mr. Lincoln felt the reasons for dropouts was too complex to discuss at the time.[7]

Adams State College in Alamosa has a high standard for training teachers and many Spanish-speaking-origin teachers graduate every year. These men and women meet the standards of the college the same as any other student. The following is a set of figures on Spanish-speaking students compiled by the registrar, Robert Showalter. It covers a

---

5
Personal interview with Mr. Gary Stephens, Central School Principal, April 25, 1967 (see appendix).

6
Personal interview with Mr. Sam Lincoln, Counselor, Alamosa High School, Alamosa, Colorado, April 25, 1967.

7
Ibid.

period of five years and indicates some trends.[8]

Campus Enrollment - Fall 1966 - 2310 students
(Indian, Hawaiian, Anglo, Foreign, and other students)
Spanish surname - 323 - approximately 14 per cent of total
enrollment.

Degrees - A.B.

	Total	Spanish Surname
Summer 1966	79	7
Spring 1966	215	25
Summer 1965	86	14
Spring 1965	178	20
Summer 1964	101	14
Spring 1964	183	29
Summer 1963	107	14
Spring 1963	202	22
Summer 1962	123	24
Spring 1962	153	17
	1,427	186 (approx. 13%)

Degrees - M.A.

	Total	Spanish Surname
Summer 1966	96	14
Spring 1966	36	5
Summer 1965	95	14
Spring 1965	40	4
Summer 1964	83	19
Spring 1964	23	2
Summer 1963	61	9
Spring 1963	19	1
Summer 1962	82	15
Spring 1962	21	1
	561	84 (approx. 13%)

---

[8] Personal interview with Robert Showalter, Registrar, Adams State College, Alamosa, Colorado, February, 1967.

A more thorough study of this information is needed. Some of the college graduates are not from Alamosa nor are they products of the Alamosa schools. A number of Alamosa High School Spanish-speaking graduates go to other colleges and vocational schools outside the San Luis Valley.

However, these figures do indicate that what Marjorie Joan Willeke discovered in her unpublished Master's Thesis is true. She found that ". . . a significant number of Spanish-speaking graduates from San Luis Valley high schools in 1963 showed academic promise in high school /but/ failed to enroll in college." She made the following recommendations:[9]

1. Groups such as elementary school teachers, guidance counselors, high school teachers, college personnel, parents, and citizens who are interested in working toward solutions, should study the problem...
2. After recommendations have been formulated, an intensive drive for publicity should be conducted. In the opinion of the writer the group should seek to educate people toward understanding the proposals.

Informed people should know that new and unfamiliar information is not heard the first time it is offered. No one can aspire to that which he does not know exists. The Spanish-speaking student will need detailed and repeated information plus help in making use of it. To this student, even filling blanks is an activity that frightens him. One unkind word will send him away. The "Anglo's" have the advantage of being in the know, they are in the have group. The Spanish-speaking students initially will need much encouragement and support.

Once these students go to college, the tendency is to complete the work for the degree. If one student from one community, neighborhood, or family succeeds then the way is open for the rest. The problem seems to be in the transition to high school from the junior high school and in the transition from high school to college. It could be that guidance and counseling programs are not meeting the needs of these students and their parents. Home room teachers may not be inspiring and challenging enough, also. Adults have a tendency to give up on an individual too soon, if they do not understand him. Every grownup person has a duty and a responsibility to help each and every youngster acquire competence in, at least, the 3-R's, because the lack of this skill will place danger at all doorsteps of the nation and the world.[10]

---

[9]
Marjorie Joan Willeke, "Follow-up Study of Graduates in the San Luis Valley High Schools." Unpublished Master's Thesis (Alamosa, Colorado: Adams State College, The Graduate Division, 1964), pp. 74-75.

[10]
Report-Educational Opportunities for Potential School and for Out-of-School Unemployed Youth-Denver Public Schools (November 30, 1963), p. c-12.

A husband and wife team, Mr. and Mrs. Donald I. Gardner, did a study at Adams State College in which they used their own Culture questionnaire as well as other testing procedures. They selected students from Manassa, Romeo, and La Jara. The Gates Survey Test and the Pinter General Ability: Non-Language Series Test were used. Seventy-two of the 101 sixth-graders tested on the Pinter had the Otis score also on their records. The results indicated that the non-language type test seemed to be quite fair. The I.Q. scores were fairly close--mean for the "Anglo's" was 99.62 and for the "Spanish" 92.25. The reading test results showed a wider gap and a more distinct one, the "Anglo's" appeared to be one-half a year ahead and the "Spanish-Americans" one-half year behind the national average. It was in the Culture test that the reasons for variation in reading skill were determined. The outstanding cause which showed up again and again was the lack of parental interest in and motivation for school activities participation.

Parents everywhere seem each day more unable to bridge the communication gap between themselves and their children. Spanish-speaking parents find their problem intensified for they see their children leaving their culture and their family behind as they grasp for the outer edges of the new culture and the new authority figures. This is a tragic circumstance and it need not be if English and Spanish are made to mutually help each other in the formation of new strong personalities.

Adult education is a coming educational area of endeavor. Already there are many programs in operation...it is in this area of education that attitudes become the primary target. The author would say that subject matter is the means by which change of attitudes for better democratic living will come about.

The adult basic education program must not be ignored. The home is the base of operations and it must be the origin of changes for the young. The parents are the logical ones to help their children. If they are poor, defeated, and ignorant, they must be helped to become a "somebody". They can change, but it will take time, effort, patience, and understanding. It will take the guided spearhead action of their children and their hopes, for parents to awaken to their own roles of constructive action. Every parent, if he is well enough, wants the best for his children. It is well to delve deeply into causes of present situations and not be blinded by superficial symptoms or biased preconceptions. To be successful in teaching, teachers must forge close bonds of mutual understanding with parents. . . this is crucial. Both teachers and parents have the opportunity and duty to continue to learn and in so doing can improve the whole area of human relationships.

There are encouraging efforts discernable in this direction of

adult basic education,[11] although, perhaps the emphasis is on the three
R's and job seeking. Important as these are, success in these will not
be achieved unless emphasis is placed in the much more difficult area
of _feeling_ and attitude changes. This is as much true of teachers as
of parents.

A Progress Report[12] from California places the estimated Mexican-
American population in the United States at over five million as of
April, 1966, and most of these people (4,500,000) live in the Southwest.
Figures for 1960 (same report) show that the education of this group is
dangerously low.

Table 1

Median Years of School Completed by Spanish Surname persons compared
with other population groups. Various age, classes, Southwest, 1960
(Males and Females Combined).

Age Group	Anglo	Spanish Surname	Nonwhite	S.S.-Anglo Gap Years	Per Cent
14 years and over	12.0	8.1	9.7	3.9	32%
14-24	11.3	9.2	10.6	2.1	19%
25 and over	12.1	7.1	9.0	5.0	41%

Frank Riesmann has stated that "children from disadvantaged homes
show less mastery of the fundamental knowledge that is helpful in all

----

11
Basic Education for Adults. A report of the California State
Committee on Basic Education, California State Department of Education,
Max Rafferty, Superintendent of Public Instruction, Sacramento: State
Committee, 1965, pp. 1-120; Tentative Outline of Basic Education and
Acculturation. Prepared by Denver Public Schools through Emily Griffith
Opportunity School. Adult, vocational, and Technical Education for Job
Opportunity Center, Inc., Denver, Colorado: Denver Public Schools,
1965; Malcolm S. Knowled, The Adult Education Movement in the United
States (New York: Henry Holt and Company, 1962), pp. 1-335; Byron E.
Chapman (Director), The Mott Basic Language Skills Program. Mott Adult
Reading Center. Flint, Michigan, Chicago, Illinois: Adult Education
Council, pp. 1-20.

12
Progress Report: Mexican-American Study Project No. 7, op. cit.,
pp. 4-9.

arts of communication."[13] Many Mexican-American or the Spanish-speaking citizens are generally speaking disadvantaged. This group joins other groups of disadvantaged. There are too many to safely ignore them.

"Suddenly we are aware that because of lack of education, know-how and, social skills, twenty per cent of the people in the richest nation in history are not equipped to live at a successful middle class standard,"[14] Dr. Catherine Nutterville reminds us. The problem is not entirely the lack of "know-how" of schools and school people in educating these masses of people. The problem has been in the lack of acceptance of the problem and realization of its urgency.

If a dedicated effort to educate the less than "nice" people is promoted in all school systems by all school personnel, the results would probably astound the world. The word dedicated assumes a mutual change of attitudes between the advantaged and disadvantaged with emphasis placed on the <u>advantaged.</u>

The truth of the matter is that this type of citizen (uneducated, non-participating, and miserable) is a threat to those who already have "arrived." It would be a mistake to redouble the efforts to educate these citizens only because of thoughts of personal safety. This is why the <u>advantaged</u> must be educated in the matter of true understanding and affection for those who are disadvantaged.

This kind of education should be a permanent broadening, continuing process, because there will always be a need for it. The Southwest, tinged with the Spanish culture of the early colonists, is still receiving fresh thrusts of today's Spanish or Mexican immigrants, the lack of English language facility remains the main obstacle to acceptance by the dominant group.

As language continues "to be primary consideration in helping citizens become participating ones," it would be well to consider the following:

> . . . no child can escape his community. . . The life of the community flows about him, foul or pure; he swims in it, drinks it, goes to sleep in it, and wakes to a new day to find it still about him. He belongs to it; it nourishes him, or starves him, or poisons him; it gives him the substance of his life. And in the long run it takes its toll of him,

---

13
Frank Riessman, The Cultivally Deprived Child (Evanston, Illinois: Harper and Row, 1962), p. 115.

14
Dr. Catherine Nutterville, "The War Against Poverty," Delta Kappa Gamma Bulletin, Volume 33 (Spring, 1967), pp. 22-23.

and all he is . . . .
The democratic problem in education is not primarily a problem of training children; it is the problem of making a community within which children cannot help growing up to be
democratic, intelligent, disciplined to freedom, reverent of
the goods of life, and eager to share in the tasks of the
age. A school cannot produce this result; nothing but the
community can do so. . . Joseph Kenmount Hart[15]

Spanish is the language of all the countries of the hemisphere
except for the United States, Canada and Brazil. Now the United
States has many people who speak Spanish and other languages, Canada's
population includes many French-speaking members, and Brazil speaks
mainly Portuguese. The English-(and only English-) speaking people of
the United States perhaps need to change from complacency to urgency
in the race for understanding. This hemisphere can be safe only if all
its members understand and know the common problems and issues of the
day. It might be well for the United States to take a look at Canada's
"bold step":

BILINGUAL CANADA

Language today can be as bitterly explosive and disruptive an
issue as either race or religion. If not handled delicately
it can threaten to tear a nation asunder, as it might have done
in India. Even in Switzerland, with its four official tongues
and rightly looked upon as a model of language harmony, there
are growing demands by a French-speaking minority that they be
allowed to break away from the predominantly German-speaking
Canton of Bern.

But in few other spots is speech a tinderier issue than in
Canada. And now, to meet the demands of its French-speaking
citizens for what they believe is their constitutional due,
the Canadian Government is apparently about to embark upon an
extremely bold step. Ottawa is said to be readying a measure
guaranteeing language rights for French-speakers outside the
Province of Quebec. The legal (and in many cases the practical)
result of this would be to make Canada a land with two offici-
ally encouraged and supported languages.

It is clear that Ottawa, after much heart-searching, has con-
cluded that this is the best way to ensure national unity. It
is felt that it will encourage French-speaking Canadians to
move more widely through the country and to become outward-
looking rather than inward-looking.

---

[15]
    Edward G. Olsen, The School and Community Reader; Education in
Perspective (New York: The MacMillan Co., 1963), p. 349.

On the other hand, the possible risks of such a policy cannot be wholly overlooked. This is a rare experiment, and runs directly counter to almost all other nations' policies, which is either to encourage a single language (as in nearly all cases) or to keep different language groups compartmentalized (as in Switzerland, Belgium, India, etc.). South Africa is one of the few lands with a policy like Canada's.[16]

Education geared to understanding and engaged in acceptance of the dignity of people is the only realistic approach to a responsible and effective future. This kind of education appears to be a world problem.

Children learn from each other and seeds for future mutual understanding are planted early in life, so segregation of Spanish-speaking children for any reason is not desirable. Groups should be able to handle both languages constructively (need not be fluent in Spanish).

As the child progresses from the first grade to the second and third and seemingly has acquired the necessary vocabulary to meet average requirements, teachers should maintain a vigilant constant awareness of blanks and voids present in this child's background of meaning. Even the most (to him) common new words being introduced daily may not have the needed meaning. He practically lives in another world (culture). The sixth grader who said, "My father is a good alligator," meant, "He is good at arguing (allegador)." The fourth grader who, when asked to make a sentence with the word consult, wrote, "Every morning I eat my eggs for breakfast con salt," was adapting what he heard to what he knew... and it was wrong. Never should a teacher laugh at a child, although any teacher can laugh with a child.

The work of implementing meanings and experiences to added vocabularies and printed symbols continues all through the school life of the student. The work of producing a citizen of the United States may need some acceptance and use of the Spanish language and culture. . . . . . teachers should be alert to the possibilities.

The Valley Courier, published at Alamosa, Colorado, carried the following Associated Press news item on page nine, Wednesday, April 26, 1967:

A second public school is going bilingual in this city with a large colony of Cuban exiles. Pupils at Central Beach Elementary School (Miami) which is evenly divided between native speakers of Spanish and English, will receive instruction in all subject-areas in both languages starting with the fall term. The program starts at kindergarten level. The

---

[16] The Christian Science Monitor. Editorial. (Thursday, August 31, 1967), p. 14.

idea is to make all pupils bilingual.[17]

The other item was concerned with Law Degree Scholarships for
Spanish-Americans, available through Ford Foundation funds at Denver
University beginning June 19, 1967.

The idea that the United States is a great nation because of the
contributions from all cultural groups needs to be reinforced con-
cretely. Too long has the idea prevailed that only the English-speaking
are responsible for the progress of this nation.

Teaching English as a foreign language which will become a primary
language takes the child as he is--Spanish, and uses what he knows to
guide him to what he ought to know. The period of reading readiness
and experiencing is an extended one. Spanish is not prohibited but
English is encouraged. The child is gradually introduced to the new
culture, but not at the expense of the old culture. Meaningful experienced vocabularies are extended in a controlled efficient manner. Skill
in listening and speaking lays the foundation for reading and writing.
The use of the senses is employed at all times, in as many variations
and contexts as possible. The respect of the child for his parents
should be carefully cultivated, this is his origin and his home base.
True, some parents may not be the best parents in the world or perhaps
they may even be completely unbearable and unworthy, but the child knows
no others and he must never be allowed to hate them. Teachers who
allowed this to happen (unwittingly as it might be) committed murder of
a "self".

> It is not logic, right facts, or 'the best', that keeps people
> sane, but a depth awareness and genuine concern for others.
> These are the goals of world harmony, the pillars of inner
> peace, the marks of an educated man.
> Should education help persons become worthy of meaningful ex-
> periences? or should education, in its competitiveness, con-
> tinue to assist people become more and more corrupt in human
> inter-relatedness?[18]

The teachers of this nation are in a strategic position to play a
decisive role during this transitional period of drastic change.
Teachers cannot shirk this responsibility.

17
The Valley Courier, "Bilingual Children" and "Law Degree Scholar-
ships for Spanish-Americans" (AP Items. Alamosa, Colorado: The Valley
Courier, April 26, 1967), p. 9.

18
Dr. Evelyn G. Rimel, "What Does it Mean to be Educated?" The
Delta Kappa Gamma Bulletin, Volume 33, No. 3 (Austin, Texas: Delta
Kappa Gamma Society, Spring, 1967), p. 29.

The materials, techniques, contents, approaches, etc., are available and usable. The tools are excellent, the artists who are using the tools are the ones that need a polishing of ideals and an increasing skill of practical application of what is known to be good.

Delving into the research necessary to produce this paper, the author is elated and strengthened by the discovery that teaching English as a foreign language which becomes a primary language has been going on in a limited unacknowledged manner since the beginning, but that the direct-on-purpose teaching of English in this way is gathering momentum today. It might be that the next step is to make English and Spanish equally important and thereby this hemisphere soon could have a bilingual population.

CHAPTER VI

SUMMARY, CONCLUSIONS, AND RECOMMENDATIONS

Summary

This study was concerned with some aspects of the teaching of English as a foreign language in Alamosa, Colorado, grades one, two, and three. The following problems were considered:

1. The tracing of the teaching of English to Spanish-speaking students.

2. The clarification of the teacher role in the process of acculturation of students coming from a "minority" group.

3. The critical analysis of three approaches to the problem.

4. The description of the city of Alamosa and its provision for the education of a specific portion of the school population.

Research in general indicated that the crux of this particular educational problem was cultural in nature. Value systems and historical backgrounds differed so much that the teaching of English to Spanish-speaking students (Spanish to English-speaking students) was more than an ordinary act of teaching factual material. The multiplicity of causes underlying this <u>emotionally</u> charged problem rejects solutions.

Bernard Valdez, who has written a history of Spanish-Americans of Denver, has this to say:

The Spanish-surnamed Coloradoan constitutes nine per cent of the state's population. Statistically he represents a disproportionate number in correctional institutions, has a high rate of juvenile delinquency, public dependency, and more significantly in school drop-outs. He is commonly referred to as the 'Spanish-American or Mexican problem' and has become the concern of every social agency.[1]

It seems necessary to emphasize the obvious fact that Spanish-speaking children are not the only ones who are considered by some to be disadvantaged and underprivileged. "It is estimated that about two-thirds of all American children come from native stock below the

---

[1] Bernard Valdez, The History of Spanish Americans (Denver: Colorado Department of Institutions, 1963), p. 7.

71

middle class or from racial and ethnic minority groups. . ."[2] (the author should question the implication of the phrase "native stock").

Also, it seems necessary to remember the W. Lloyd Warner statement, "ninety per cent or more of our teachers are from the middle class."[3] To try to reconcile these two very pertinent and important educational challenges is the problem of the century. It becomes urgent that teachers at all levels strive to protect the children who do not fit the present culture climate of the school.

The author believes that the positive approach is the best; no one needs to be told that he is disadvantaged and underprivileged. This approach "saves face." The poor know that they are poor, they know that many specific major unmet needs make them unhappy and ill, they know that they have not and that other more fortunate people do have. For far too long a time the poor (underprivileged and disadvantaged) have listened to words and promises and much too often have efforts to help them resulted in only short sporadic glimpses of what "might have been."

In the past, continued disappointments created a way of life that protected itself from further hurt by passive acceptance of existing conditions, but today the passive acceptance is changing to non-informed, aggressive and destructive violence. Words, promises, and short-lived measures are not believed any more.

The poor need hope arousal by immediate, sustained and continued constructive action. It is going to take time for the hope to revive and the poor are entitled to this time. It is not by stressing their disadvantaged and underprivileged state that the poor may be motivated toward a better life, it is by stressing their personal worth as individuals and as citizens of this nation that they will truly respond.

The summation of data presented in this paper seems to point out the educator lack of full awareness of the significance of the attitudinal gap between students and teachers in particular and among people in general. It seems, then, that all adults should combine forces to better understand the role of attitudes in the promotion of human understanding.

---

[2]
Harold W. Bernard, Psychology of Learning and Teaching (New York: McGraw-Hill Book Company, 1965), p. 374.

[3]
W. Lloyd Warner, American Life: Dream and Reality (Chicago: The University of Chicago Press, 1953), pp. 176-180.

Conclusions

The author has arrived at the following conclusions:

1. Human beings are human beings regardless of their many complex and differentiated inherited traits, characteristics, situations, conditions, and states. It appears that the main task of teachers is to make human beings more <u>human</u>.

2. Spanish-speaking students act differently because of their cultural history but they are not necessarily inferior or basically different. They have certain imperative <u>needs</u> that must be met quickly, naturally, and correctly. It is possible for them to learn just like any other human being learns.

3. It seems urgent that the people of the world today and tomorrow should utilize the native language of an individual as a tool <u>for</u> learning.

4. Improvement in people to people understanding calls for uncloudy thinking, sincere commitment, and, at times, judicious use of anxiety.

The teaching of English to Spanish-speaking individuals without destroying their innermost concept of self should strengthen the prospects for a much better world and a more exciting future.

Recommendations

On the basis of this study the following recommendations are suggested to aid in the process of teaching Spanish-speaking students to become full participating first-class citizens of an English-speaking United States. It could be that the United States could prove to other nations of the world that the matter of language enrichment can prevent later serious misunderstandings due, in part, to deeply rooted attitudes fostered by initial disrespect to native languages.

These recommendations might be added to the information file at Catholic University of America:

1. Education of adults is imperative. Parents must be helped to recover their father and mother role. They need to recognize how important they are to themselves, to their children and to the world itself. Parents have first priority to their children's love and with this love the great privilege and duty to <u>teach</u> them well.

2. Teach English to the Spanish-speaking students <u>in addition</u> to their own language. Make known to these students the

possible avenues of great service to all people because
they have two languages. Teach Spanish to the English-
speaking. Make the United States, at least, bilingual.

3. Support the teaching of what a democratic government has
    done and what it can do. Narrow the distance between
    the "creed and the practice."

4. Insure, postively, for every youngster the opportunity
    <u>to know</u>, <u>to be</u>, and <u>to contribute</u>.

5. Emphasize action, deeds, and involvement. Awaken a
    realization of the urgency of person to person and people
    to people commitment to world understanding.

APPENDICES

APPENDIX I

MATERIALS COLLECTED BY EVA R. BORREGO

SOME LANGUAGE DIFFICULTIES

APPENDIX I

MATERIALS COLLECTED By Eva R. Borrego

(Courtesy of Adams State College)

SOME LANGUAGE DIFFICULTIES

The most important first step in the many series of steps to be taken by the Spanish-culture background student is the desperate and immediate need for a fluent and correct command of the English language. Sympathetic understanding has been shown in the valuable work that has been done in the development of reading readiness programs and in the vocabulary-building methods for these children.[1]

But very little work has been done to help students with their enunciation and pronunciation problems; yet, the Spanish language differs greatly from the English language in this respect.

The peculiar English enunciation and pronunciation difficulties of the Spanish-culture background student seriously divide the one group of students from the other. It is imperative that Spanish-culture background students should quickly and efficiently learn to correctly enunciate and pronounce the English language. This chapter is devoted to a detailed study of this one problem.

The purpose of this study is to determine (1) what the most

_____

1. Dwight Hamilton, Teaching English and Reading to Non-English Speaking Children, Denver: Inter-American Workshop, Denver University, May 1945.

   Marie Hughes, Teaching A Standard English Vocabulary With Initial Reading Instruction, New Mexico: issued by State Department of Education, 1936.

   Learning English Incidentally: A Study of Bilingual Children, Bulletin 1937, No. 15, U.S. Dept. of Interior, Office of Education, Project in Research in Universities, Washington, D.C.; Government Printing Office, 1938.

   Successful Practices in Teaching of English to Bilingual Children of Hawaii, Bulletin 1937, No. 14, Washington, D.C.; Government Printing Office, Office of Education.

   We Learn English, The San Jose Experimental School, Albuquerque, New Mexico: University of New Mexico, 1936.

common errors of English enunciation and pronunciation are; (2) under-standings of cause-effect relationships which produce the errors; (3) ways of evading, if possible, such errors, and (4) suggested remedies that might be successful in lessening time and effort expended in the teaching of correct enunciation and pronunciation to boys and girls whose mother tongue is Spanish. This study could be quite technical and complicated but a determined effort has been made to keep it as practical as possible for the use of busy homeroom school teachers.

Data on errors were derived largely from (1) general observation for a number of years; (2) personal experience; (3) specific observa-tion in case study work with special emphasis given to oral reading and conversation; (4) books, magazines, bulletins, and papers on the sub-ject.

Some of these causes will overlap each other, but, in general, findings may be summarized as follows:

1. Articulation

   A. The chief cause of poor enunciation lies in the
      articulation of vowels and combinations of vowels.
      The Spanish vowels and semivowels:[1]

              a--a in padre--car
              e--e in eso--lesson
              e--e in ser--separator
              i--i in pido--picaresque
              o--o in hora--ornate
              o--o in flor--core
              u--u in luna--lute
              i--i in aire--I   semi-
              u--u in causa   vowels
                    ow in cow

      These are produced by a definite dropping and moving
      of the lower jaw. The facial muscles, relaxed and
      facile, produce pronounced expressions. The English
      vowels:[2]

              ee-e in me
              i--i in it

---

1. Tomas Navarro and Aurelio H. Espinosa, A Primer of Spanish Proun-ciation, p. 13, Chicago: Benj. H. Sanborn & Co., 1927.

2. Nemoy-Davis, The Correction of Defective Consonant Sounds, p. 31, Boston: Expression Company-Publishers, 1937.

```
ay--ay  in day
e--e    in met
a--a    in care
a--a    in cat
ir--i   in bird
a--a    in amid
u--u    in up
oo-oo   in boot
oo-oo   in book
oh-o    in note
aw--a   in tall
o--o    in stop
ah-a    in father
```

as a rule can be articulated without a dropping of the lower jaw. The face need not show much expression. Whenever vowels, semivowels or combinations of vowels in English enunciation are produced by a moving and dropping of the lower jaw, the enunciation is nearly always correct. There is a tendency to pronounce short vowels as long vowels:

```
stop--stohp
brush--brahsh
finger--finghr
oven--ohven
it--eet
ball--bahll
book--book
       boot
```

In Spanish all the vowels of a word have a clear quality and are not slurred as is often done in English. There-fore, children will need to learn to sound certain com-binations of vowels by slurring them:

```
chair       bounce
fair        because
stair       people
pounce      saucepan
```

Special drills for vowel pronunciation will overcome many deficien-cies along that line.

Short vowel key words:[1]

---

1. Anna Dorothea Cordts, The Word Method of Teaching Phonics, P. 7, Chicago: Ginn and Co., 1929.

candy	dust
pans	run
sack	jump
hands	bunny
bag	supper
man	hot
lantern	pocket
rattle	box
kitty	helpers
big	beg
will	seven
pitcher	fence
hill	pencil
dishes	letter
fifteen	tent
hungry	

Note:
Ask pupils to watch your lips as you pronounce the words clearly
and distinctly. If the room is quiet, as it should be for all
work in phonetics, there is no need of exaggerating the sounds
in order to make them clearly audible.[1]

B. Possible remedial work

1. Songs to condition facial muscles:

a.   I'M AN OLD COWHAND

Step a-side you or-ner-y Ten-der-feet
Let a big back buch-er-oo past
I'm the tough-est hom-bre you'll ev-er meet--
Tho' I may be the last. Yes-sir-ree
We're a van-ish-ing race. No-sir-ree can't last long--
Step a-side you or-ner-y Tenderfoot,
While I sing my song--

Cho.
I'm An Old Cow-hand--from the Ri-o Grande--
But my legs ain't bowed--an my cheeks ain't tanned--
I'm a cowboy who nev-er saw a cow,
Nev-er roped a steer 'cause I
don't know how, and I sho' ain't
fix-ing to start in now.
Yip-py-I-O-Ki-Ay, Yip-py-I-O-ki-Ay.

---

1. Ibid. p. 16.

I'm an Old Cow-hand--from the Ri-o Grande--
And I learned to ride--'fore I learned to stand--
I'm a rid-in' fool who is up to date,
I know ev-'ry trail in the Lone Star State,
'cause I ride the range in a Ford V-Eight
Yip-py-I-O-Ki-Ay, Yip-py-I-O-Ki-Ay.

b.   SKIP TO MY LOU

Lost my girl, now what will I do;
Lost my girl, now what will I do;
Lost my girl, now what will I do?
Skip to my Lou, my darling.

Cho.
Skip, skip, skip to my Lou;
Skip, skip, skip to my Lou;
Skip, skip, skip to my Lou;
Skip to my Lou, my darling.

c.   PLAY BALL[1]

Play ball, play ball,
Everyone likes to play ball,
Sometimes you catch it and sometimes you miss,
But when you miss remember this:

Let the ball roll, let the ball roll,
No matter where it may go;
Let the ball roll, let the ball roll,
It has to stop sometime, you know.
Play ball, etc.........

2. Poems - Jingles

PIN LORE[2]

See the pin and pick it up
All the day you will have luck;
See a pin and let it lay,   (pick, pin, luck)
You'll have bad luck all that day.

---

1. Gerald Marks and Rose O'Neil, Sing a Song of Safety, New York:
   Irving Caesar, 1936.

2. B. A. Botkin, editor, A Treasury of American Folklore, pp. 79-791,
   foreword by Carl Sandburg, New York: Crown Publishers, 1944.

Needles and pins!
Needles and pins!   (needles)

FIFTY FROGS

Fifty frogs a jumping
Fifty frogs I saw
Fifty frogs a jumping   (fifty)
Fifty frogs I saw.   (fifty)

THE BEE

What does the bee do?
Bring home honey.
What does father do?
Bring home money.
What does mother do?
Pay out money.
What does baby do?
Eat up the honey.

-------Christina Rossetti

SEVEN TIMES ONE ARE SEVEN

I am so old, so old I can write a letter;
My birthday lessons are done.
The lambs play always, they know no better.

(birthday - birsday)

HEY DIDDLE DIDDLE

Hey diddle diddle
The cat and the fiddle
The cow jumped over the moon,
The little dog laughed,
To see such a sport
And the dish ran away with the spoon.

FIDDLE DEE DEE

Fiddle dee dee, Fiddle dee dee,
The fly has married the bumble bee.

KNOW YOUR LESSON

Know your lesson with expression?
They ask me everywhere.

        (Lesson, everywhere)
I know my lesson with expression!
I answer with a glare. (glare)

3. Choral Speech[1]

  John Cook has a little grey mare,
  (Hee, haw, hum)
  Her back stood up and her bones
  they were bare, (Hee, haw, hum)
  John Cook was riding up Shooter's
  bank, (hee, haw, hum)
  And here his nag did kick and
  prank, (Hee, haw, hum)
  John Cook was riding up Shooter's
  hill, (Hee, haw, hum)
  And his mare fell down and made her
  will, (Hee, haw, hum)
  The saddle and bridle she laid on the shelf.
  If you want any more you can sing it yourself.

WHISTLE, WHISTLE, OLD WIFE

"Whistle, whistle, old wife, and
you'll get a hen."
"I wouldn't whistle," said the wife,
"If you could give me ten."
"Whistle, whistle, old wife, and
you'll get a cock."
"I wouldn't whistle," said the wife,
"if you gave me a flock."
"Whistle, whistle, old wife, and you'll
get a gown."
"I wouldn't whistle," said the wife,
"for the best one in town!"
"Whistle, whistle, old wife, and you'll
get a man."
"Wheeple, whaupple," said the wife,
"I'll whistle if I can!"

---

1. S. Keppie, Teaching of Choric Speech, Boston: Expression Co., undated.

II. Tongue Placement

A. Tongue placement is another important factor in producing the right enunciation. The Spanish spoken in the Southwest does not employ the <u>th</u> sound. Children do not know where to place their tongues to produce such a sound, so they will say:

> tread for thread
> tree for three
> tank for thank
> tick for thick

The final <u>d</u> is often not heard although it is sounded, as in:

> climbed, told

Children will also confuse c, s, and z sounds, because in Spanish the tongue placement is almost identical. In English for these sounds, the tongue is placed differently in each case. The word <u>cinco</u> has two sounds, so has the word <u>concern</u>. Children like to hear similarities as well as differences.

B. Possible Remedial Work

1. Voice Exercises:

2. Game - THREAD THE NEEDLE

Have the children sitting in a circle. Have a large needle and some thread. Count three and let someone thread the needle. Count three and repeat:

One, two, three
Thread the needle,
Thank you, thank you!

For breath sound as in "thank" place tongue against the back of the upper front teeth and force the air through. For the voice sound, place the tongue in the same position as for the breath sound but force the voice through.

III. Air Release

A. The s, z and c sounds can be controlled by regulating the air release, thus:

decision - decizion
policeman - polizeman
chicken - shicken

By the time a child learns to say chicken, he meets up with the word machine and the teacher starts all over again.

B. Possible Remedial Work

1. Making sounds
Escaping steam from a tea kettle makes a buzzing noise like this:z-z-z-z-z-z.

To make these sounds place the tongue back of the upper four front teeth, bring the jaws almost together, the space between the upper and lower teeth is very small. The s sound is a breath sound...the z is voiced.

2. Tongue twisters
"Dis" - this
Thelma thanked them for the thimble.
Thirteen thirsty thrushes flew through the thicket.

Way down in Arkansas, I saw a saw that sawed the best of any saw I ever saw saw. Father saw the same saw and he said it sawed the best of any saw he ever saw saw.

She sells sea shells down by the seashore. (Repeat)

3. Stories

The Story of Chicken-Licken
(Ending of Story)

"But Fox-lox took them into the fox's hole and he
and his young ones soon ate up poor Chicken-licken,
Henny-penny, Cocky-locky, Ducky-lucky, Draky-laky,
Goosey-loosely, Gander-lander and Turkey-lurkey,
and they never saw the king to tell him that the
sky had fallen!"

IV. Explosives

A. Work on explosive sounds is necessary because Spanish is
not an explosive language. The English explosives are
p, b, t, d, ch, j, k, and g.

B. Possible Remedial Work

1. Tongue twisters

A big black bug bit a big black bear.
3 times
Peter Piper picked a pack of pickled peppers.
3 times
Tiny Tommy touched the ticklish tiger.
3 times
Do dandy doings daringly.
3 times

2. Poem

FURRY BEAR

If I were a bear
  And a big bear too,
I shouldn't much care
  If it froze or snew: (snowed)   (poetic expression)
I shouldn't much mind
  If it snowed or friz   (froze)
I'd be all fur-lined
  With a coat like his!
                          -----A. A. Milne

FINGER POEM

Five little rabbits went out to walk
They liked to boast as well as talk.
The first one said, "I hear a gun!"

The second one said, "I will not run."
Two little ones said, "Let's sit in the shade."
The big one said, "I'm not afraid!"
Bang, Bang! went a gun,
And the five little rabbits run.

3. Rope skipping rhyme:

TEDDY BEAR

Teddy bear, teddy bear, turn around;
Teddy bear, teddy bear, touch the ground;
Teddy bear, teddy bear, tie your shoe;
Teddy bear, teddy bear, now skidoo!

V. Lip Placement

A. Lip placement drills will tighten the facial play of
muscles. English enunciation is so much tighter than
Spanish. People who have mastered the English language
usually speak with clear-cut enunciation that reveals a
conscious tightening of facial muscles. The b and v,
the m and n are excellent letters for lip placement
exercise.

B. Possible Remedial Work

B and v need special drill. The Spanish sound for these
is almost the same............(Lobato-Lovato)

1. Jingle

Be very, very good,
Naught do not be! (repeat)

Show how the lips must be together, how the air is
pushed out to make the sound of the b.

Show how the upper teeth fit over the lower lip to
produce the v sound.

Veryily, veryily, veryily, (repeat)
Button, button--Who has the button?

2. Music.

Use musical voice-exercises substituting the following:

moo............ moo ....
nu............. nu .... na .... na ....
boo........... boo ....
voo........... vo .... voo ....

87

3. Sentences

   Make up a story about Betty and Vera

VI. Unfamiliar letter sounds

   A. Children rarely have a working knowledge of the letter
      sounds h and w. As a separate sound the Spanish h is
      silent; the w has a double u sound. However, the English
      h and the Spanish j have much in common. The w causes
      such mixups as having a fricative consonant, i.e. g-w,...
      agua becomes agwa (double u sound), ...bueno becomes gueno,
      and eventually woman becomes gooman!

   B. Possible Remedial Work

      To make the sound of w, fix the lips as if for whistling,
      and force the voice through. (Whistle songs)

      1. Songs

                  THE WINDMILL[1]

         At the setting of the sun,
         The windmill's day is done.
         The bells softly peal,
         The neighbors come for meal,
         Then homeward run
         To bake a crusty bun!
                              (use of peal for ring, and the
                               sound of both peal and meal.)

                  SANCTUS[2]

         Holy, holy, holy, merciful and mighty,
         Holy, holy, holy, holy is the Lord!
         Wonder, love and glory, shine from sea to sea.
         Holy, holy, holy, holy Lord is he.

      2. Tongue twisters

         How much wood would a woman willingly bring? (repeat)

         One woman, two women, one woman, two women,
         One woman, one hundred women.

---

1. Marguerite V. Hool, G. Gildersleeve, H. Leavitt, and C. Kirby, Singing
   Days, The World of Music series, p. 94, New York: Ginn and Co., 1944.

2. Marguerite V. Hood, et al., On Wings of Song, pp. 11-16.

VII. Accent

A. All Spanish accent is important, stressed accent is
extremely important. The Spanish ear is sensitive and
likes to hear accentuations. Many children will accen-
tuate English words only because the habit of stressing
is so powerful. Boys and girls will also accent English
words that have the same spelling as Spanish words, for
example:

        animal --- animal
        hospital - hospital
        papa ----- papa
        mamma ---- mamma
        doctor --- doctor

Let children discover the cause of difference in sound.

B. Possible Remedial Work

1. Sentences

        A dog is an animal. (mention other animals)
        Many animals help us.
        Hello papa. (father)
        Hello mamma. (mother)
        My papa and my mamma showed me an animal hospital.
        There was a doctor in the hospital.

2. Rope skipping rhymes[1]

        I told ma,
        Ma told pa;
        Johnny got a lickin'
        Hee, hee, haw!
        Salt, vinegar,
        mustard, pepper. (Gradual increase of speed)

VIII. Attuning the ear to English sounds.

A. Countless errors are made because the ear is not attuned
to English sounds. The difference in sound is not heard.
A child hears the correct pronunciation of the word cream
but he hears and repeats crem. Poor enunciation of the
following words is due largely to lack of ear training in
English sounds:

---

1. Ibid. (6).

```
hill      -    heal
this      -    these
quit      -    quiet - quite
of        -    off
```

B. Possible Remedial Work

    1. Contrast

        a.   <u>Hill</u>

            Jack and Jill
            Went up the hill
            To get a pail of water, etc.

            <u>Heal</u>

            Heel, toe,
            One, two, three.
            Heal, toe,
            And one, two, three.

        b. Finger play

            <u>This</u>

            These are mother's forks and knives
            And this is mother's table.
            This is sister's looking glass
            And this is baby's cradle.

        c. Jingles

            <u>These</u>

            These five books belong here,
            These four books belong there,
            Here, there, everywhere!

            <u>Ship</u>

            I saw a ship a sailing,
            A sailing in the sea.
            And, oh, it was all laden,
            With pretty things for thee.

            <u>Sheep</u>

            Baa, baa black sheep
            Have you any wool?

d. Sentences

<u>Of</u> - <u>Off</u>

"Take care of the baby."
The book fell off.

IX. Sentence Rhythm

A. In Spanish there is a sentence rhythm of accentuation as well as a word rhythm. Sometimes the children are pronouncing the words correctly but the sentence rhythm produces a strange sound-effect of the whole articulation. Positive teaching of a correct habit of speaking is required. Making a child self-conscious is destructive. Choral speech is immensely useful.

B. Possible Remedial Work

1. Student participation

a. Active games

Pum, Pum Pull Away
Run Sheep Run
Touch Football
Volley Ball

b.. Singing games

Farmer in the Dell
London Bridge is Falling Down
Blue Bird Through My Window
A Tisket A Tasket

c. Dramatizations

Jack and Jill
Three Bears
Red Riding Hood
Three Little Kittens
Three Pigs

d. Music

(1) Action songs
I See You
How Do You Do My Partner
Hickory, Dickory, Dock

<pre>
          (2) Rounds
               Frere Jacques - Brother John
               Three Blind Mice
               Scotland's Burning

          (3) Other Songs
               Little Jack Horner
               My Home's in Montana
               Country Gardens

          (4) Rhythm band
               Accented music

     e. Speech

          Conversation
          Planning
          Sharing

     f. Choral Speech

          Poems that fit the specific needs.

     g. Listening - Intelligent Audience -
          Attuning the Ear

          (Told, read or sung)
          Stories
          Poems
          Anecdotes
          Riddles
          Descriptions
          Jingles
          Songs
</pre>

In teaching clear enunciation, the teacher proceeds from the known to the unknown. The teacher should know the child's past experiences, background, immediate environment and heritage. In this study, all this necessary teacher-knowledge hinges on the fact that another language was involved. If the teacher knows, can anticipate, can provide remedies for probable errors before those same errors happen, then significant progress is achieved.

To know what causes poor enunciation is necessary; to do something about it is wise; to follow up the actual functioning of a new language is the essence of real teaching. Good teachers everywhere, regardless of community types, individual differences, or grade levels, should unobtrusively yet constantly strive for good enunciation and pronunciation.

Here is a sample list of enunciation demons, all of which fall under one or more of the nine named causes:

address	balloon	blood
advising	bath	bring
animal	bathe	brush
arithmetic	been	butter
ball	big	button
candy	mouth	their
cereal	Mrs.	clothes
chair	napkin	come
chewing	naughty	cough
chicken	needle	curtain
choose	snake	danger
church	some	describe
cloth	sour	dessert
fur	squeeze	diamond
give	stable	dish
goes	stand	does
grandmother	stair	dough
grieve	state	dream
juice	saw	drink
jump	steak	eat
language	stink	error
leather	stitch	evening
lemon	succeed	everybody
lettuce	sugar	excused
lightening	sum	everywhere
lives	sweater	family
little	swim	feed
machine	swing	feet
meat	syrup	fifth
Miss	telephone	oatmeal
mother	thank	whether
of	ship	whiskers
off	these	whistle
once	thick	fill
onion	things	finger
oven	thousand	food
pasture	thirsty	foreign
people	thread	forsake
pick	three	funny
pint	throw	shoes
play	thunder	show
please	together	sickness
policeman	tomato	sidewalk
potato	tongue	sing
precious	trousers	sister
puddle	turkey	window
putty	twelve	with
saucepan	twist	yellow
reading	uniform	yesterday
scissors	vase	you
scratch	vegetable	yours
sheep	weigh	

93

APPENDIX II

(From an Unpublished Thesis - permission given)

"PROCEDURES FOR TEACHING ENGLISH TO BILINGUAL
CHILDREN AS A BASIS FOR READING PRACTICES"

By Mary Jane Jiron

From an Unpublished Thesis - Permission Given

"PROCEDURES FOR TEACHING ENGLISH TO BILINGUAL CHILDREN AS A BASIS FOR READING PRACTICES"

By Mary Jane Jiron

Most authorities agree that the bilingual child should have a speaking vocabulary of from 400 to 500 words before they begin reading. As a conclusion to this chapter, the writer has compiled a list of words that may be used by new teachers as a source of reference for guidance in teaching vocabulary words to bilingual children.

The following list of words was compiled from four sources. They are as follows:

1. "Standard Minimal Speaking Vocabulary for Pre-First Grade" (Compiled by the San Jose Training School).

2. "Vocabulary for Beginners" (Compiled by Fresno County Project, Fresno, California).

3. "Basic Speaking Vocabulary", Teachers Guide to Education of Spanish-Speaking Children, Bulletin No. 14, California State Department of Education, Sacramento, 1952, pp. 46-50.

These lists were compared with:

4. "The Dolch Basic Sight Vocabulary List" and 95 Common Nouns" which includes words that make up 59 to 75% of all reading matter in school subjects.

This list includes both sight words and words that bilingual children should know. The writer has tried to indicate the source of each word. Some words were listed only in one list, but were included because the writer knew from experience that children will need to know them. For example, Tireman left out "which"; Dolch included it. There are words as "tractor" or "squirrel" that were not included in all the lists. The teacher should adapt this list to her own particular need.

Code

1. Words that are unmarked are included in all lists.

2. If a word is included only in three lists it is indicated by *. The letter in parenthesis indicates which list did not include this word.

3. Letters in parenthesis without * indicates the lists in which that particular word is included.

4. What letters indicate:

D--Dolch list
F--Fresno County list
T--Tireman list (San Jose Training School)
C--California Education Department list (Bulletin No. 14)

a
about* (D)
after
afternoon
again
air (T)
airplane
all
almost
alone (T)
along (T)
already (T)
always (C,F)
am
an* (F)
and
another (T)
any (T,D)
anything (T)
apple
are
arm
around
ask
as (D)
at
automobile (C,T)
away
baby
bad* (D)
Christmas (T,D)
church (T)
circle (T,C)
clap* (D)
clay (D,C)
clean* (D)
clock* (D)
clothes (T)
coat
cold
color
comb* (D)
come
cook (F)

back (T)
bag (T)
ball
banana (C)
basket* (D)
bath* (D)
bat (C)
bean (F)
bear* (F)
because (D)
bed
be
been (D,T)
before (D,F)
begin (C,F)
bell
best (T,D)
better (T,D)
big
bird
birthday
black
block (F)
blow* (D)
blue
boat* (F)
bath
box
bow (T)
boy
bread
end* (D)
erase (F)
eraser (F)
every (D)
everyone (F)
excuse me* (D)
eye
face
fail
family (F)
farm (T,D)
farmer (C)
far (D)

breakfast
bring
broom (F)
brother
brought
brown
brush (C,F)
build (T,F)
bus (F)
but (D,T)
butter* (D)
buy
by* (C)
cake
call (T,D)
care (T)
came
can
candy
cap (C,T)
car
carrot (C)
carry
cat
catch* (D)
cent (F,C)
chair
chalk (F)
chicken
children
choose (F)
good morning
got
grandfather* (D)
grandmother* (D)
grass
great (T)
green
ground
grow
guess (T)
had
hair
half (T)

96

corner (T)
corn (T, D)
cough (F)
count (F)
cover (F)
cow
crayon* (D)
cross (F)
cry* (D)
cup* (D)
daddy* (D)
dance (T)
dark* (D)
day
dear (F, C)
did
different (T)
dime (F)
dinner (T,C)
dirty* (D)
dish* (D)
does
dog
doll
dollar (F)
done
don't
do
deer
down
draw
dress
drink
drum
dry* (D)
egg
eight
just (T, D)
kind* (F)
kite* (F)
kitty* (F)
knees* (D)
knife* (D)
know
ladies (T)
late* (D)
lay (T)
laugh
learn
leaf* (D)
left
leg

fast
food (F)
feet (F)
father
field (F)
find
finger* (D)
fingernail* (D, T)
fire (T)
first
fish* (D)
five
fix
flag
floor
flower
fly
fodd* (D)
found
four
friend (F)
from
front (T)
fruit
full (T, D)
fun* (D)
funny
game
garage* (D)
garden
gave
get
girl
give
glad
go
goes
going
good
good by
must* (F)
myself
nail* (D)
name
near
neck
need* (D)
nest* (F)
never
new
next* (D)
nickel (F)

hall* (D)
hammer* (D)
hand
handkerchief (F,C)
happy
hard (T,D)
has
hat
have
head
hear* (D)
he
hen (C)
head
hello* (D)
her
here
hide* (D)
high* (D)
him
his
hit* (D)
hold
hole
horn (T)
home
hop (F)
horse
hot
how* (C)
hurt* (C)
I
ice cream (F)
if
I'll
I'm
in
into (F)
is
it
its
jump
people
piano* (D)
piece
pig
pink (T)
place (F)
plant (F)
plate* (D)
playground (F)
please

let	night	pocket
letter	nice	poor (T)
lie* (D)	nine	potato
light	noise (T)	pretty
like	no	pull
line (F)	nose	purple
listen	nothing	put
little	not	puzzle (F)
live	now	quiet (F)
long	number	rabbit
look	o'clock	rain
lost	of	ran
lot (T)	office (F)	read
love	off	ready
lunch	old	recess (F)
made	oh	red
make	on	rest (T, D)
mail (F)	one	ride
men	once* (F)	right
many (C, T)	onion (T)	ring (T, F)
marbles (C)	only* (F)	road
may (T, C)	open	rock* (D)
me	or	roll* (D)
meat* (D)	orange* (D)	room
mean (T)	other	rooster
men	our	rope (F, C)
might	out	round
milk	outside	run
mine (T)	over	said
minute	own (T, D)	Santa Claus (T, C)
money* (D)	page	same* (D)
moon (T, F)	paint* (D)	sand (F)
more	pair* (D)	sang
morning	pan* (D)	saw
mother	pants (F)	sat
mouth	paper	say
mouse (T)	park (T)	school
move* (D)	party	scissors* (D)
much	pencil	seat (C, T)
music	pennies	see
set	sweep (F)	seen
seven	swim (T)	sell (T, F)
saw (T)	swing* (D)	send (T, F)
shall* (F)	table	up
she	tail (T)	us
sheep (C)	talk	use
shelf (F)	take	very* (F)
shirt* (D)	teacher (T, D)	wagon
shoe	tooth (T, D)	wait
should (T)	tear* (D)	wake
show	tell	wall (T, C)
shut	ten	walk
sick	thank you* (D)	want

98

sing
sister
sit
six
sky
skipsmall (T, D)
sleep
side (T)
slice (C)
snow (T, D)
soap* (D)
so* (F)
socks (F)
still (T)
stockings (T, C)
soft
some
something* (D)
sometime (T)
song
soon* (F)
spot (T)
spoon* (D)
squirrel (C)
stand
stay (T)
start (D, T)
stick* (D)
stop
store* (D)
story (T, F)
stove* (D)
straight (T, C)
straw* (D)
street
string
such (T)
summer (C, T)
sun

supper (T, C)
suppose (T)
sweater (T)
than
then
the
their
them
there
those
they
thing
thing* (F)
this
those
three
thought (T)
through
throw
tie
till
time
to
toss* (D)
today
together (T)
toilet* (D)
tomorrow* (D)
toothbrush
top
towel* (D)
town* (D)
toy
tractor
train* (D)
tree
truck (F)
try
turn

two
uncle (T)
under
until
warm
watch (T)
was
wash
water
way
wear
we
will
we'll (T)
went
were
wet (T)
what
when
white
which
whole (T)
who
why
wind
window
winter (T)
wipe (F)
wish (T)
woman* (D)
work
would
write
year (T)
yellow
yes
yesterday (F)
you
your

APPENDIX III

A TEACHING UNIT

OUR PUBLIC SCHOOLS

APPENDIX III

A TEACHING UNIT

OUR PUBLIC SCHOOLS

CENTRAL SCHOOL ELEMENTARY GRADE

Teacher, Miss Eva R. Borrego

TEACHING PHILOSOPHY:

The child is the important factor. Understand the child's
heritage and environment; value his experiences. Teach
the child.

TABLE OF CONTENTS

GRADE. . . . . THIRD
TIME . . . . . . SIX WEEKS
STUDENTS . . . 37 . . . ALL ABILITIES . . . SPANISH AMERICAN

1. OBJECTIVES

A. CENTRAL:

The Ability to appreciate Our Public School as a normal living experience.

2. CONTRIBUTORY:

1. An attitude toward Our Public School which will lead to ready and effective learning.

    (a) The conviction that good Public Schools are the natural heritage of all boys and girls, regardless of race, wealth, or health.
    (b) Some knowledge of what constitutes a good Public School.

2. The ability to accept the fact that because man craved knowledge, primitive life progressed.

3. The ability to understand and accept the fact, that as society became more complex, the need for education became more pronounced.

4. A general knowledge of the history of:

    (a) Origin of Schools
    (b) Private Schools
    (c) Public Schools
    (d) Specialized Schools
    (e) Coeducational Schools
    (f) Folk Schools
    (g) Vocational Schools

5. Know the task of the:

    (a) Teacher
    (b) Principal
    (c) Superintendent
    (d) Board of Education

6. Knowledge of Public Schools in our State.

7. Knowledge of all other Schools in our State.

    (a) Higher learning
    (b) Specialized

103

8. Knowledge of sources of income for Public Schools.

9. Acquaintance with all schools in our city.

10. An appreciation of the great privilege which we have of attending Our Public Schools.

C. INDIRECT:

1. A desire to read, to learn new words.

2. A desire to discover the best of the past and the best of the future.

3. A desire for moral effort and discipline.

4. To develop admiration of the just, not the strong.

5. Awaken a thirst for research.

   (a) Questioning at home
   (b) Looking for pictures or stories to prove a point
   (c) Learn to use the Public Library.

6. Discover the fact that our hands are useful.

   (a) Illustrate facts
   (b) Picture beauty
   (c) Build miniature structures for better solving of problems.
   (d) Mold with clay. . carve with soap . . use rulers, saws, brushes, etc.

7. Know individuals by sharing tools, not weapons.

8. Learn that Spelling is absolutely essential.

9. Know that:

   (a) Other people have opinions.
   (b) Honest work is happiness.
   (c) Leisure time is invaluable.
   (d) Personal competence, freedoms and adequacy are precious.

10. Develop tolerance:

    (a) In thinking
    (b) In planning
    (c) In action

11. PRESENTATION. . .MOTIVATION

A. Must be based on children's experiences.

    1. Any day some child will have an experience to share with the group about Schools.

        (a) A trip ...a story by grandfather...a picture.
        (b) A group excursion.
        (c) Attending a culmination program given by some other grade on Schools...etc.

III. PRETEST

A. Present a very simply worded test on Objective B..I..(b)

B. A need for more knowledge discovered. Let's go!

IV. COMMITTEE GROUPS

All work shared and interchanged.

A. Gathering information

    1. Reading

    2. Interviews.

    3. Home questionnaire

    4. Group discussions

    5. Pictures

    6. Listening to lectures

    7. Museum

    8. Painting

    9. Building

    10. Demonstrations.

B. Each committee responsible for:

    1. A finished illustrated book:

        (a) Stories to be correctly written, watch:

　　　　　　(1)　Punctuation. . . Spelling
　　　　　　(2)　Structure . . . English and Sentences

2.　At least an addition of 100 words for oral and written
use. . . flash-card words to be made, drilled and
checked by some member of committee.

3.　At least an addition of 25 words for Spelling. . . word
list made, drilled and checked by some member of committee.

4.　At least 10 Arithmetic problems arising out of committee
work.

5.　Some contribution to general knowledge and enjoyment of
class.

　　　(a)　A play
　　　(b)　Illustrated stories
　　　(c)　A moving picture . . . slides
　　　(d)　A puppet show
　　　(e)　A demonstration lesson with vocabulary words
　　　(f)　A demonstration lesson with Spelling words
　　　(g)　Costumes

6.　All committees to:

　　　(a)　Edit a daily paper
　　　(b)　Keep bulletin board posted
　　　(c)　Use maps and charts

VI.　DESIRABLE HABITS AND ATTITUDES

A.　Habits and attitudes to be drilled and practiced at all times.

　　1.　Habits:

　　　　(a)　Honesty...truthfulness...obedience...preseverance
　　　　(b)　Attentiveness...alertness
　　　　(c)　Courtesy...promptness
　　　　(d)　Neatness...orderliness
　　　　(e)　Individual concentration...never mind others
　　　　(f)　Personal cleanliness
　　　　(g)　Good posture
　　　　(h)　Safety consciousness
　　　　(i)　Enjoy work...hard work

　　2.　Attitudes:

　　　　(a)　Pride in personal achievement...pride in personal
　　　　　　appearance...pride in all surroundings.

        (b) Satisfaction in only the best effort.
        (c) Helpfulness to others...kindliness...sportsmanship.
        (d) Initiative...weighing of facts...thoughts, ideas,
            results and effects...then purposefull action.
        (e) Respect for:

            (1) Self
            (2) Individuals
            (3) Property
            (4) The common good

VII. POSSIBLE TYPES OF CULMINATIONS

A. Programs prepared by group for:

    1. Other grades

    2. Parents

    3. Clubs

B. Compile, bind and present to the Library a:

    1. Book

    2. Play

C. Have open house for whole school

VIII. TESTING

A. Test on all objectives

B. Test on all desirable habits and attitudes

C. Use as many types of testing procedures as possible:

    1. True and false

    2. Multiple choice

    3. Filling blanks

    4. Yes and no.

                    etc.

IX-X. EVALUATION

A. Using the measuring rods of:

      1. Tests

      2. Graphs

      3. Other teachers' opinions

      4. Scales

      5. Nurse's opinion

      6. Mother's opinion

HAVE WE,

      LEARNED THAT GOING TO SCHOOL IS NORMAL LIVING?

TENTATIVE VOCABULARY

(Checked with Gates Word List
(Third Grade Level)

correct
brick
teach
learn
library
obey
Adams State Teachers' College
everyone
through
education
safety
taxes
student
clubs
knew
rules
laws
children
people
could
chimney
nerves
dangerous
holiday
their
old fashioned
because
transportation
wrong
pioneers
understanding
exercise
politeness
courtesy
normal

flag
study groups
college
taught
modern
free
path
sportsmanship
tile
rough
buildings
principal
teachers
graduation
telephone
high school
superintendent
accident
food
either
solve
germs
bought
picnic
there
buses
chief
reason
enemies
country
manners
carefulness
prepare
enjoy

(Can be added to or subtracted from.)

TENTATIVE SPELLING LIST

they	dress	log cabin
the	same	not
have - has	past	teach
there-their	long	school
is - are	ago	study
these - this	rules	laws
high	snow	horseback
tired	prayers	houses
seem	those	faded
teacher	letters	quill pens
samplers	knit	spin
aid	made	make
bench	rough	hard
cold	lunch	after
taught	early	girls
saw	cook	ride
buggy	few	farm
work	hard	tools

(SUBJECT TO CHANGE)

BIBLIOGRAPHY

A. BOOKS

Abrams, Charles. Forbidden Neighbors. New York: Harper Brothers, 1955.

Adamic, Louis, From Many Lands. New York: Harper Brothers, 1940.

Ahmann, Stanley, et. al. Evaluating Elementary School Pupils. Boston: Allyn and Bacon, Inc., 1960.

Anderson, Paul. Language Skills in Elementary Education. New York: The Macmillan Company, 1964.

Andersson, Theodore. The Teaching of Foreign Languages in the Elementary School. Boston: D. C. Heath and Company, 1953.

Beals, Ralph L. and Humphary, Norman D. No Frontier to Learning: The Mexican Student in the United States. Minneapolis: University of Minnesota Press, 1957.

Beardslee, David and Michael Wertheimer. Readings in Perception. New York: D. Van Nostrand and Company, Inc., 1958 (Reprint, 1965).

Bellows, F. L. The Techniques of Language Teaching. London: Longman's Green, Inc., 1961.

Benedict, Ruth. Patterns of Culture. 18th Printing with an Introduction by Franz Boas and a new Preface by Margaret Mead. New York: The New American Library of World Literature, Inc., 1960.

Bernard, Harold W. Human Development in Western Culture. Boston: Allyn and Bacon, Inc., 1962.

Bettelheim, Bruno. The Informed Heart. New York: Free Press, 1960.

Boatright, Mody C., et. al., Texas Folks and Folklore. Dallas, Texas: University of Dallas, 1954.

Boliti, Leo. The Mission Bell. New York: Scribners and Sons, 1953.

Bond, Guy I. and Eva Bond Wagner. Teaching the Child to Read. Fourth edition. New York: The Macmillan Company, 1966.

Braddy, Haldeen, Cock of the Walk. Albuquerque: University of New Mexico Press, 1955.

Brameld, Theodore. Education for the Emerging Age: Newer Ends and Stronger Means. New York: Harper and Row Publishers, 1965.

Brauner, Charles J. and Hobert W. Burns. Problems in Education and Philosophy. Foundation Series. Englewood Cliffs, New Jersey: Prentice-Hall, Inc., 1965.

Brembeck, Cole S. Social Foundations: A Cross-Cultural Approach. New York: John Wiley and Sons, Inc., 1966.

Brengelman, Frederick H. and John C. Manning. Linguistic Capacity Index. Fresno, California: The Authors, 1964.

Brooks, Melvin S. The Social Problems of Migrant Farm Laborers. Carbondale, Illinois: Southern Illinois University, Department of Sociology, 1960.

Brown, Ina Corrine. Understanding Other Cultures. Englewood Cliffs, New Jersey: Prentice-Hall, Inc., 1963.

Buber, Martin. I - Thou. Second edition. New York: Scribners, 1958.

Buchanan, Cynthia Dee. Teacher's Guide to Programmed Series One and Two. Sullivan Associates, Webster Division. New York: McGraw-Hill Book Company, 1964.

Buental, J.F.T. The Search for Authenticity. New York: Holt, Rinehart and Winston, 1965.

Bumpass, Faye L. Teaching Young Students English as a Foreign Language. New York: American Book Company, 1963.

Burma, John H. Spanish-Speaking Groups in the United States. North Carolina: Duke University Press, 1954.

Buros, Oscar Krisen (ed.). The Third Mental Measurements Yearbook. Hiland Park, New Jersey: Cryphon Press, 1939.

Caplovitz, David. The Poor Pay More. New York: Free Press of Glencoe, 1963.

Carrell, Theresa and V.J. Kennedy. Preschool Instructional Program for Non-English Speaking Children. Foreword J.W. Edgar, Commissioner of Education. Austin: Texas Education Agency, April, 1960.

Chapman, Byron E. (Director). The Mott Basic Language Skills Program. Mott Adult Reading Center, Flint, Michigan. Chicago, Illinois: Allied Education Council, n.d.

Cline, Marion, Jr. Improving Language Arts of Bilingual Through Audio-visual Means. Las Vegas, New Mexico: New Mexico Highlands University, 1962.

Cole, Stewart Grant and Margaret Cole Wiese. Minorities and the American Promise. New York: Harper and Brothers, 1954.

Conant, J.B. Science and Common Sense. New Haven, Connecticut: Yale University Press, 1951.

Cook, L.A. Inter-Group Education. New York: McGraw-Hill Book Company, 1954.

Cronbach, Lee J. Educational Psychology. New York: Harcourt, Brace and Company, 1954.

Cunningham, C.S.C., Ph.D. The Pivotal Problems of Education. New York: The Macmillan Company, 1960.

Dawson, Christopher. The Crisis of Western Education. New York: Sheed and Ward, Inc., 1961.

Dawson, Mildred A. and Georgiana Collis Newman. Language Teaching in Kindergarten and Elementary Grades. New York: Harcourt, Brace and World, Inc., 1966.

Dechant, Emerald V. Improving the Teaching of Reading. Englewood Cliffs, New Jersey: Prentice-Hall, Inc., 1964.

De Onis, Jose. The United States as Seen by Spanish-American Writers. Boulder, Colorado: The University of Colorado, 1954.

Devlin, Joseph. A Dictionary of Synonyms and Antonyms. New York: Popular Library, Inc., 1961.

Dewey, John. Democracy and Education. New York: The Macmillan Company, 1916.

De Witt, M.E. Let us Recite Together: Silent Dust, Rodon, The Pyramid. We Consecrate Ourselves to Work, and Other Selections. Poughkeepsie, New York: The Artcraft Press, 1935.

Dolch, Edward William. Psychology and Teaching of Reading. Second Printing. Champaign, Illinois: The Garrard Press, 1951.

Doll, Ronal C. Curriculum Improvement: Decision-making and Process. Boston: Allyn and Bacon, Inc., 1965.

Doty, Gladys G. and Janet Ross. Language and Life in the U.S.A.: American English for Foreign Students. New York: Harper and Row, Publishers, 1960.

Eby, Frederick. The Development of Modern Education. Second Edition. New York: Prentice-Hall, Inc., 1952.

Ells, Walter Crosby. American Dissertations on Foreign Education. Committee on International Relations. Washington, D.C., U.S.A.: National Education Association of the United States, 1959.

Feleach, R.F. Why Johnny Can't Read and What you Can Do About It. New York: Harpers, 1955.

Finocchiaro, Mary. Teaching English as a Second Language. San Francisco: Henry Holt and Company, 1963.

Fletcher, Harvey. Speech and Hearing in Communication. New York: D. Van Nostrand Company, Inc., 1961.

Foshay, Arthur W. and Kenneth D. Wann. Children's Social Values. New York: Columbia University, 1954.

Frances, Arlene. That Certain Something. New York: Dell Publishing Company, 1960.

Frazier, Alexander. A Program for Poorly Languaged Children. Columbus, Ohio: The Ohio State University, College of Education Center for School Experimentation, October, 1963.

Fries, Charles C. Linguistics and Reading. New York: Holt, Rinehart and Winston, 1963.

Gardner, John W. Excellence: Can We Be Equal and Excellent Too? New York: Harper Colophon Books, Harper and Row, Publishers, 1961.

Gattegno, Caleb. Background and Principles: Words in Color. Chicago, Illinois: Learning Materials, Inc. (a Subsidiary of Encyclopaedia Britannica, Inc.,), 1964.

Gilson, Etienne. A Gilson Reader: Selections from the Writings of Etienne Gilson. Edited with an Introduction by Anton C. Pegis. Garden City, New York: Image Books, a Division of Doubleday and Company, Inc., 1957.

Graham, Jory. Handbook for Project Head Start. New York: Anti-Defamation League of B'nai B'rith, 1955.

Gray, William S. On Their Own in Reading. Revised edition. Chicago, Illinois: Scott, Foresman and Company, 1960.

Greene, Harry A. and Walter T. Petty. Developing Language Skills in the Elementary Schools. Second edition. Boston: Allyn and Bacon, Inc., 1963.

Hafen, L.R. and A.W. Hafen. Old Spanish Trail. Glendale: Arthur H. Clark Company, 1955.

Hall, Edward T. The Silent Language. A Premier Book. New York: Fawcett World Library, 1963.

Havighurst, Robert J. The Public Schools of Chicago. Chicago: The Board of Education, 1964.

Hay, Julie, et. al. Reading with Phonics. Revised edition. Philadelphia: Lippincott, 1960.

Hefferman, _____ (Chief). A Guide for Teachers of Beginning Non-English-Speaking Children. Sacramento: California State Printing Office, 1932.

Heilman, Arthur W. Principles and Practices of Teaching Reading. Columbus, Ohio: Charles E. Merrill Books, Inc., 1961.

Hemphill, Irene E. (Ed.). Choral Speaking and Speech Development. Darien, Connecticut: Educational Publishing Corporation, 1945.

Harter, Helen. English is Fun or the Rhythm and Song Approach to the Teaching of English to Non-English-Speaking Beginners. Second edition. Tempe, Arizona: Helen Harter, 1962.

Herr, Selma E. General Patterns of Effective Reading Programs. Dubuque, Iowa: Wm. C. Brown Company, Publishers, 1963.

Kemp, Barbara H. The Youth We Haven't Served: A Challenge to Vocational Education. Washington, D.C.: United States Government Printing Office, 1966.

Kibbe, Pauline. Latin Americans in Texas. Albuquerque: University of New Mexico Press, 1946.

Kneller, George P. Educational Anthropology. New York: John Wiley and Sons, Inc., 1965.

Kneller, George P. Introduction to Philosophy. New York: John Wiley and Sons, Inc., 1964.

Knowles, Malcolm S. The Adult Education Movement in the United States. New York: Henry Holt and Company, 1962.

Kolesnik, Walter B. Educational Psychology. New York: McGraw-Hill Book Company, Inc., 1963.

Krug, Edward. The Shaping of the American High School. New York: Harper and Row, 1964.

Lado, Robert. Language Teaching: A Scientific Approach. New York: McGraw-Hill Book Company, Inc., 1964.

Lado, Robert and C.C. Fries. Monographs for Teaching English as a Second Language: English Pattern Practices; English Pronunciation Lessons in Vocabulary; English Sentence Patterns. Ann Arbor: University of Michigan Press.

Landis, Paul H. Rural Life in Progress. New York: McGraw-Hill Book Company, 1940.

Latting, Lucile H. and Grant H. Vest. Helping the Retarded Reader. Denver: Colorado Department of Education, 1955.

Leen, Edward. What is Education? New York: Sheed and Ward, 1944.

Leighton, Roby E. (Coordinator) Workshop for Teachers of Bilingual Students. Bulletin, Tucson, Arizona: University of Arizona Press, 1961.

Levenson, Sam. Everything but Money. New York: Simon and Shuster, Inc., 1949-1966.

Lewis, Oscar. The Children of Sanchez. New York: Random House, Inc., 1961

Loomis, Louis Ropes. (ed.). Aristotle on Man and Universe: Metaphysics. Parts of Animals, Ethics, Politics, Poetics. New York: Walter J. Black, 1943.

Madsen, William. The Mexican-Americans of South Texas. New York: Holt, Rinehart and Winston, 1964.

Manuel, H.T. The Education of Mexican and Spanish-Speaking Children in Texas. Austin: The University of Texas, 1930.

Marden, Charles F. Minorities in American Society. New York: American Book Company, 1952.

Martin, Walter G. Teaching Children Who Move with the Crops. Fresno, California; Fresno County Superintendent of Schools, 1955.

Mayer, Martin. The Schools. New York: Harper and Brothers, 1961.

Mazurkiewicz, Albert J. New ITA Books Early to Read Series. New York: Initial Teaching Alphabet Publications, Inc., 1964.

Meredith, Patrick. Learning, Remembering and Knowing. New York: Association Press, 1961.

Mehl, Marie A. et. al. Teaching in Elementary School. Third Edition. New York: The Ronald Press Company, 1965.

Meyer, Albert Cardinal (Archbishop of Chicago). Lenten Pastoral Letter. Chicago: Committee for Migrant Workers, 1962.

Montessori, Maria. The Montessori Method. New York: Frederick A. Stokes Company, 1912.

Moras, Frank. Yonder One World: A Study of Asia and the West. New York: The Macmillan Company, 1958.

Morris, Van Cleve (ed.). Becoming an Educator: An Introduction by Specialists to the Study and Practice of Education. Boston: Houghton Mifflin Company, 1963.

Mort, Paul R. and William S. Vincent. Introduction to American
    Education. New York: McGraw-Hill Book Company, Inc., 1951.

MacRae, Margit W. Teaching Spanish in the Grades. Boston: Houghton
    Mifflin Company, 1957.

McCausland, Margaret et. al. Speech Through Pictures. Drawings by
    Louise Robertson Pfieffer. Ninth Printing. Magnolia, Mass.:
    Expression Company, 1961.

McClosky, Gordon et. a. Introduction to Teaching in American Schools.
    New York: Harcourt, Brace, and Company, Inc., 1954.

McCracken, Glenn et. al. Basic Reading. Preprimer I-I and Workbook
    I-I. Illustrated by Carol Kitzmiller and George Wilde. New
    York: J.B. Lippincott Company, 1963.

McWilliams, Carey. North from Mexico. Philadelphia: J.B. Lippincott
    Company, 1949.

Navarro, Tomas and Aurelio M. Espinosa. A Primer of Spanish Pronunciation.
    New York: Beng H. Sanborn and Company, 1926.

Nesbitt, Phil. Nicolas Patatiesa. Chicago: Wilcox and Follett Company,
    1944.

Olsen, Edward G. The School and Community Reader: Education in
    Perspective. New York: The MacMillan Company, 1963.

Olson, Willard C. Child Development. Second edition. Boston: D.C.
    Heath and Company, 1959.

Ortega y Gasset, Jose. The Revolt of the Masses. New York: W.W.
    Norton and Company, 1960.

Packard, Vance. The Status Seekers. New York: The David McKay Company,
    Inc., 1959.

Parker, Jayne Hall. My Speech Workbook: (Book I) A Remedial Workbook
    for the "S" and "Z" Sounds. Danville, Illinois: The Interstate
    Printers and Publishers, Inc., 1961.

Passow, A. Harry (ed.). Education in Depressed Areas. New York:
    Teachers College, Columbia University Press, 1963.

Pei, Mario. Language for Everybody: What It Is and How to Master It.
    New York: The Devin-Adair Company, 1956.

Peiffer, James E. Cultural Background of Americans of Mexican Descent.
    Toledo, Ohio: Toledo Diocesan Councils of Catholic Men and Women,
    1962.

Penfield, Wilder and Lamar Roberts. Speech and Brain Mechanisms.
    Princeton, New Jersey: Princeton University Press, 1959.

Piaget, Jean. La Langue et la pensee Chez l'enfant. (Neuchatal:
    Delachaux et Niestle, 1924-5). Trans. The Language and Thought
    of the Child. New York: Harcourt, Brace and Company, Inc., 1932.

Pounds, Ralph L. and James B. Bryner. The School in American Society.
    Second edition. New York: The Macmillan Company, 1967.

Prator, Clifford H. Language Teaching in the Philippines. Philippines:
    United States Educational Foundation in the Philippines, 1950.

Pritchett, Victor S. Spanish Temper. New York: Alfred A. Knopf,
    Publisher, 1954.

_____. Psychology of Learning and Teaching. Second edition. New
    York: McGraw-Hill Book Company, 1965.

Read, E. Lee and M. Benjamin. Historia Ilustrada De Nuevo Mexico.
    Santa Fe, New Mexico: Compania Impresora Del Nuevo Mexico, 1911.

Redden, John D. and Francis A. Ryan. Intercultural Education. School
    of Education Fordham University. Milwaukee: The Bruce Publishing
    Company, 1951.

Richards, I.A. Basic English and Its Uses. New York: W.W. Norton and
    Company, Inc., 1943.

Riessman, Frank. The Culturally Deprived Child. Evanston, Illinois:
    Harper and Row, 1962.

Robinett, Ralph F. A Linguistic Approach to Beginning Reading for
    Bilingual Children. Boston: D.C. Heath and Company, 1965.

Roessel, Robert A. (ed). San Carlos Apache Papers: Indian Education
    Center. Tempe, Arizona: Arizona State University, 1964.

Rose, Charles E. Curriculum Guide for Elementary Schools. Santa Fe,
    New Mexico: The State Board of Education, 1950.

Ruch, Floyd L. Psychology and Life. Sixth edition. Chicago: Scott,
    Foresman and Company, 1963.

Salzman, Leon and Jules H. Masserman. Modern Concepts of Psychoanalysis.
    New York: Philosophical Library, Inc., 1962.

Saunders, Lyle. Cultural Differences and Medical Care: The Case of
    the Spanish-Speaking People of the Southwest. New York: Russell
    Sage Foundation, 1954.

Schoolfield, Miss and Miss Timberlake. The Phonovisual Method. Washington 16, D.C.: Phonovisual Products Inc., 1959. Monograph.

Schubert, Delwyn G. and Theodore L. Torgerson. Improving Reading in the Elementary School: A Handbook Emphasizing Individual Correction. Dubuque, Iowa: Wm. C. Brown Company, Publishers, 1963.

Shane, Harold G. et. al. Beginning Language Arts Instruction With Children. Columbus, Ohio: Charles E. Merrill Books, Inc., 1961.

Shere, Marie Orr. Speech and Language, Training for the Palsied Child at Home. Danville, Illinois: The Interstate Printers and Publishers, Inc., 1961.

Shermis, S. Samuel. Philosophic Foundations of Education. American Book Company, 1967.

_____. Slums and Suburbs. New York: McGraw-Hill Book Company, 1961.

Spencer, Herbert. Education, Moral and Spiritual. London: G. Manwaring, 1861.

Spencer, Frank C. Colorado Story. Denver: The World Press, Inc., 1924.

Silverman, Susan B. Selected Annotated Bibliography of Research Relevant to Education and Cultural Deprivation. Chicago: University of Chicago, 1964.

Smith, Louis M. and Bryce B. Hudgins. Educational Psychology: An Application of Social and Behavioral Theory. New York: Alfred A. Knopf, Publisher, 1967.

Smith, Marion F. Teaching the Slow Learning Child. New York: Harper and Row Publishers, 1954.

_____. Spanish-Speaking Children of the Southwest: Their Education and the Public Welfare. Austin: University of Texas, 1965.

Stack, Edward M. The Language Laboratory and Modern Language Teaching. New York: Oxford University Press, 1960.

Strickland, Ruth G. The Contribution of Structural Linguistics to the Teachers of Reading, Writing, and Grammar in the Elementary Grades. Bloomington, Indiana: Indiana University, 1963.

Sutton, Elizabeth. Knowing and Teaching the Migrant Child. Washington, D.C.: Department of Rural Education of NEA, 1960.

Swenson, John H. Learning on the Move: A Guide for Migrant Education. Denver, Colorado State Department of Education, 1960.

_____. Teacher's Guide for We Learn English. New York: American Book Company, 1963.

_____. Teaching and Learning English as a Foreign Language. Ann Arbor: University of Michigan Press, 1945.

Terman, Lewis M. (ed.). Genetic Studies of Genius. Volume I. Mental and Physical Traits of a Thousand Gifted Children. California: Stanford University Press, 1959.

Thomas, Charles Kenneth. Handbook of Speech Development. New York: The Ronald Press Company, 1956.

Tidyman, Willard F. Teaching the Language Arts. Second edition. New York: McGraw-Hill Book Company, Inc., 1959.

Tinsley, Willa Vaughn (ed.). Music Activities for Latin-American Children in the Elementary Grades. San Marcos, Texas: Southwest Texas Teachers College, 1944.

Tireman, L.S. Teaching Spanish-Speaking Children. Albuquerque: University of New Mexico Press, 1948.

Tireman, L.S. and Mary Watson. A Community School in a Spanish-Speaking Village. Albuquerque: University of New Mexico Press, 1948.

Trauger, William K. Language Arts in the Elementary Schools. New York: McGraw-Hill Book Company, 1963.

Tuck, Ruth D. Not with the Fist. New York: Harcourt, Brace and World, Inc., 1946.

Ulibarri, Horacio. The Effect of Cultural Differences in the Education of Spanish-Americans. Albuquerque: The College of Education, University of New Mexico, 1958.

Ulibarri, Horacio. Social and Attitudinal Characteristics of Migrant and Ex-Migrant Workers: New Mexico, Colorado, Arizona, and Texas. Albuquerque: The College of Education, University of New Mexico, 1965.

Ulich, Robert. Philosophy of Education. New York: American Book Company, 1961.

Valdez, Bernard. The History of Spanish Americans. Denver: Colorado Department of Institutions, 1963.

Valentine, Charles Wilfred. Psychology and Its Bearing on Education. Bungay, Suffolk, Great Britain: 36 Essex Street. Strand Ex 2., Richard Clay and Company, Ltd., 1960.

Vaugh, Loren and Staff. Teachers Guide for the Teaching of Reading: Reading Curriculum Development Program. Phoenix, Arizona: Phoenix Elementary Schools, District I, Maricopa County, 1959.

Wallrich, William Jones. The Strange Little Man in the Chile Red Pants. Fort Garland, Colorado: Cottonwood Press, 1949.

Warner, W. Lloyd. American Life: Dream and Reality. Chicago: The University of Chicago Press, 1953.

Whittenburg, Clarice T. and George I. Sanchez. Materials Relating to the Education of Spanish-Speaking People: A Bibliography. Austin: The University of Texas Press, 1948.

Wolfe, Doyne and J. Henry Owens. Handbook for Teachers of Spanish in the Elementary Grades. Department of FLS, Ypsilanti: Eastern Michigan University, 1961.

Wolfe, I. and M. Fullerton. Together We Sing. Chicago: Wilcox and Follet Company, 1952.

Woods, Sister Frances Jerome. Cultural Values of American Ethnic Groups. New York: Harper and Brothers, 1956.

B. BOOKS: PARTS OF SERIES

Hughes, Ann et. al. Language Arts: Beginning Reading for Disadvantaged Children. Hegeler Project. Open Court Basic Readers Series. La Salle, Illinois: Open Court Publishing Company, 1964-1965.

McKee, Paul, et. al. Reading for Meaning Series With Section in Teacher's Guide. Introducing English: An Oral Pre-Reading Program for Spanish-Speaking Primary Pupils by Louise Lancaster. Boston: Houghton Mifflin Company, 1966.

Simpson, Elizabeth. SRA Better Reading Books. Series, Grades 5-6-7-8, 9-10. Chicago: Science Research Associates, Inc., 1962.

Stansfield, Russell N. The Human Side of Teaching. Volume XXXVIII. May, 1961.

C. PERIODICALS

Adler, Manfred. "A Study of the Effects of Ethnic Origin on Giftedness," The Gifted Quarterly, 7 (Autumn, 1963), 98-101.

Anderson, Margaret. "After Integration - 'Higher Horizons,'" Time, Volume 112 (April 21, 1963), 10.

Ausubel, David P. "Teaching Strategy for Culturally Deprived Pupils: Cognitive and Motivational Considerations," School Review, Vol. 71, 1963.

Bagdikian, Ben H. "The Invisible Americans," Saturday Evening Post, Vol. 236 (December 21-28, 1963), 27-28.

Baynham, D. "Great Cities Projects," Journal of the National Education Association (April, 1963).

Berube, Maurice R. "The Urban School: Education and the Poor," The Commonweal, Vol. 86 (March 31, 1967), 46.

Bettelheim, Bruno. "The Decision to Fail," School Review. Vol. 69, Winter, 1961, 377-412.

_____. "Teaching of the Disadvantaged," Journal of National Education Association (September, 1965), 8-12.

Beyer, Evelyn. "Montessori in the Space Age?" Journal of the National Education Association, Vol. 52 (December, 1963), 36, 38.

Blum, Virgil, S.J. "The Negro Child-Twice Deprived," Ave Maria, Vol. 105 (April 1, 1967), 30.

Bolander, Don (Director). "How to Gain Command of Good English," Career Institute (1962), 14.

Borrego, Eva R. "The American Child with a Two Language Heritage," National Elementary Principal, Vol. 25 (June, 1946), 33-34.

_____. "Life Takes on New Meaning," Rural Life and Education (March, 1951), 13, 14-17.

Brady, Agnes M. "Spanish in the Elementary Schools," Hispania. 45 (1962), 95-110.

Brameld, Theodore. "Intercultural Democracy--Education's New Frontier," The Educational Forum, 12 (November, 1947).

Brameld, Theodore and Edward B. Sullivan. "Anthropology and Education," Review of Educational Research, AERA (February, 1961), 80-79.

Bree, G. "Double Responsibility of the Foreign-Language Teacher: Proficiency in the Language and Mastery of the Literature and Culture." Publications of the Modern Language Association, 78 (May, 1963), 6-10.

Brookover, Wilber B. and David Gottlieb. "Sociology of Education," Review of Educational Research, 31 (February, 1961), 51.

Burton, William H. "Education and Social Class in the United States," Harvard Educational Review, 23 (Fall, 1953), 250.

Campa, Arthur. "Languages Pack a Global Wallop," Rocky Mountain News (February, 1958), Editorial Page.

Carroll, James P. "A Plant Shuts Down," Ave Maria, 99 (January 25, 1964), 8.

Carrow, Sister Mary Arthur. "Linguistic Functioning of Bilingual and Monolingual Children," Journal of Speech and Hearing Disorders, 21-23 (September, 1957). 371-380.

Carson, Roy M. and Jack M. Thompson. "The Joplin Plan and the Traditional Reading Groups," Elementary School Journal, LXV (October, 1964), 27.

Chavez, Simon J. "Preserve Their Language Heritage," Childhood Education, 33 (December, 1956), 165-185.

Chavez, Simon J. and Twila Lee Erickson. "Teaching American Children from Spanish-Speaking Homes," Elementary School Journal, 47 (1957).

Ching, Doris C. "Effects of a Six Month Remedial English Program on Oral Writing and Reading Skills of Third Grade Hawaiian Children," Journal of Experimental Education. 32 (Winter, 1963), 103.

_____. "Methods for the Bilingual Child," 42 (January, 1965), 17.

Coleman, Algernon and Barbara B. King. "Part II, The Course of Study: Summaries and Analyses," English Teaching in the Southwest; Organization and Materials for Instruction of Spanish-Speaking Children, American Council on Education (1940), 61-63.

Cowen, Robert. "The Prosperity Gap is Widening," Christian Science Monitor, Second Section (Monday, April 10, 1967).

Cutts, Warren. "Special Language Problems of the Culturally Deprived," Clearing House, 37 (October, 1962), 80-83.

_____. "Reading UNreadiness in the Underprivileged," Journal of the National Education Association (April, 1963), 23-24.

Daugherty, Louise G. "Working With Disadvantaged Parents," Journal of the National Education Association, 52 (1963), 18-20.

Denny, Terry. "Montessori Resurrected: Now What?" Educational Forum, 29 (May, 1965), 436-441.

Dos Passos, John. "The Spaniards Were Here Before Us," Readers Digest (June, 1957), 215-219.

Downing, John and Ivan Rose. "The Value of ITA: We are Enthusiastic,"
and Cutts, Warren G. "It's Too Soon to Know Definitely," Journal
of the National Education (September, 1964), 21-22.

Dunne, John Gregory. "Strike!" Saturday Evening Post, 240th Issue
(May 6, 1967), 40, 32-68.

Clementine, Sister Marie. "Program for the Culturally Deprived Youth
With Academic Potential," National Catholic Association Bulletin,
62 (August, 1965), 378-281.

Elder, Neil B. "We're Really All One Crowd," Journal of the National
Education Association (July, 1954), 410-412.

Espinosa, Carmen. "Music Since Coronado," The New Mexico Magazine
(August, 1962), 21-41.

Fieldhusen, John F. "Taps for Teaching Machines," Education Digest,
28 (May, 1963), 17.

Finch, Alice. "After Graduation--What Then?" The Delta Kappa Gamma,
24 (Summer, 1958), 5-14.

Foster, Dorothy and Clarence M. Williams. "Aural-Oral Written Versus
Aural-Oral in Teaching Spanish to Fourth Graders," Modern
Language Journal, 44 (April, 1960), 153-157.

Freeland, Alma M. "Helping Parents Understand," The National Elementary Principal, 35 (September, 1955), 240.

Freeman, Dr. "A Report on the 1959 Summer Language Institutes,"
Hispania. 43 (March, 1960), 56-61.

Friggens, Paul. "Is the Negro Equal in Intelligence and Ability?"
Readers Digest, Condensed from PTA Magazine, 84 (March, 1964), 83-87.

Frum, Barbara. "Our Unspoken Language," Condensed from Chatelaine,
The Catholic Digest, 31 (January, 1967), 116-120.

Fuller, C. Dale. "The International Understanding We Seek," Colorado
School Journal, 69 (February, 1954), 4.

Furbay, John H. "The Challenge of Education for One World," 70,
Colorado School Journal (December, 1954), 12-15, 26-27.

Gallagher, James and William Rogge. "Talent and the Culturally Disadvantaged," 36, Review of Educational Research (February, 1966),
51-55.

Gannon, Thomas M. "Harlem's Immortal Five Per Cent," America, 115
(August 27, 1966), 208-210.

Gans, Herbert J. "Doing Something About Slums," Commonweal, 23 (March 18, 1966), 688-693.

Getzels, Jacob W. and P.W. Jackson. "A Study of Giftedness," The Gifted Student, United States Department of Health, Education and Welfare, Monograph No. 2, Government Printing Office, 1960, 1-18.

Gilmore, Kenneth O. "Laredo Learns About the War on Poverty," Readers Digest, 90 (January, 1967), 44-49.

Glover, Katherine. "New Spurs to Community Action," Parent's Magazine, 36 (August, 1961), 62.

Gooden, Opal. "How to Speak English to Foreigners," America, 1 (April, 1949), 26-32.

Graham, E. Ellis. "Facts and Alibis on the School Drop-Out Problem," Colorado School Journal, 79 (December, 1963), 11-12.

Griffen, Lee. "Henry Gonzales of Texas," Catholic Digest, 27 (October, 1963), 83-87.

Grinder, Robert E., Aiko Otomo, and Winifred Toyoto. "Comparisons Between Second, Third, and Fourth-Grade Children in the Audio-Lingual Learning of Japanese as a Second Language," Educational Research, 6 (December, 1962), 191-198.

Gross, Cordelia Baird. "To Teach is to Love," Readers Digest, 67 November, 1955), 35-39.

Hakes, David T. "Psychological Aspects of Bilingualism," Modern Language Journal, 49 (April, 1965), 227.

Hallett, Paul. "Film Shows Exploration in Colorado by Pioneers," Southern Colorado Register, (Friday, July 17, 1962), 1.

Handlin, Oscar. "Live Students and Dead Education," Atlantic, 208 (September, 1961), 29-34.

Hefferman, Helen. "Teaching English as a Second Language to Elementary School Pupils," Visalia (March, 1962), 1-21.

Hooper, Bayard (ed.). "Crisis of the Individual: Modern Society's Growing Challenge--A Provocative Ne Series-Part I," Life, 62 (April 21, 1967), 67-68.

Jacobs, John F. and Marell L. Pierce. "Bilingualism and Creativity," Elementary English, 43 (May, 1966), 499-500.

Jesen, Vernon J. "Effects of Childhood Bilingualism," Elementary English, 39 (February, 1962), 132.137.

Johnston, Marjorie. "Language Needs in Government," Reprint from School Life (April, 1957), in Colorado Congress of Foreign Languages Bulletin (October, 1957), 11.

Kennedy, John F. "The President's Message on Education," Higher Education, 29 (March, 1963), 3-12.

Kenworthy, Leonard S. "Education for the Community of 1985," Educational Leadership, 18 (May, 1960), 470-474.

Keston, Morton J. and Jimenez, Carmine. "A Study of Performance on English and Spanish Editions of the Stanford-Binet Intelligence Test by Spanish-American Children," Journal of Genetic Psychology, 85 (February, 1954), 263-269.

King, Lulu. "Peaceful Solutions to World Problems," Colorado School Journal, 70 (January, 1955), 25.

Klineberg, Otto. "Life is Fun in a Smiling Fair-Skinned World," Saturday Review, 46 (February 16, 1963), 75-87.

Kreye, George W. "Foreign Languages in the Elementary Schools," Modern Language Journal, 39 (May, 1955), 258-261.

Larew, Leonor A. "FLES in Puerto Rico," Hispinia 46 (May, 1963), 384-387.

Lloyd, Jean. "Developing Creativity with the Culturally Deprived," Instructor, 75 (February, 1966), 27, 131-133.

Lockmiller, David A. "A University President in the Far East," 39 (December, 1953), 531.

Lopez, Ruben. "Language Laboratory," Audio-Visual News: Arizona Association for Audio-Visual Education, 1 (March, 1962), 4.

Malik, Charles H. "The Foreign Alumnus," Association of American Colleges Bulletin, 39 (December, 1953), 611-617.

Martin, William E. "Gee, I'm Glad We're All Different," Journal of the National Education Association, 63 (April, 1954), 219-220.

_____. "Values Too, Can Cause Discrimination," Educational Leadership, 12 (November, 1954), 90-93.

Miller, Bernard S. "Working With Gifted Students from Disadvantaged Homes," Bulletin of National Association of Secondary School Principals, 50 (April, 1966), 166-174.

Mueller, Klaus. "The U.S. Army Language School," Education Digest, 27 (January, 1962), 1-64.

Murchland, Bernard G. "The Case Against God," Commonweal, 75 (October, 1961), 111-112.

McCracken, Glenn. "The Newcastle Reading Experiment," Elementary School Journal, 54 (March, 1954), 385-390.

McGrath, Earl J. "Language Study and World Affairs," School and Society, 75 (May 31, 1952), 348.

McJenkins, Virginia. "Atlanta-Fulton County Program Prepares New Readers," Delta Kappa Gamma Bulletin, 28 (Winter, 1962), 22-30.

McKenzie, Bill. "Miss Gibson Believes Language Bars Understanding of Latin Americans," Pueble Chieftain, Daily (Tuesday, September 4, 1962), 3A.

McRill, Paul C. "The Foreign-Language Program and How to Tell it from the Old One," Colorado School Journal, 79 (January, 1964), 19-22.

Nibling, Phyllis. "Montessori: Learning to Learn," Contemporary: Denver Post (February 6, 1966), 18-21.

Nutterville, Catherine. "The War Against Poverty," Delta Kappa Gamma Bulletin, 33 (Spring, 1967), 22-23.

Ogle, Alice. "Gallegos and Some Spanish-Speaking Realities," Ave Maria, 101, (January 30, 1965), 10-13.

Parker, B. Ford. "Enrichment in School Libraries," Childhood Education, 39 (February, 1963), 290-293.

Pattillo, Manning M. "Resolving the Conflict of Purpose Between the Search for Truth and the Teaching of Values," Current Issues in Higher Education: Higher Education Reflects on the Larger Society, Smith, G. Kerry (ed.),(1966), 113.

Raths, Louis. "Sociological Knowledge and Needed Curriculum Research," in James B. MacDonald (ed.), Research Frontiers in the Study of Children's Learning, (1960), p. 21.

Redbird, Helen Marie. "A Pilot Study to Indicate the Possible Success of Using Standardized Test in Determining the Learning Potential or Intelligence of the Children of Domestic Agricultural Migrant Workers in Colorado," Colorado State Department (Denver: 1961), Mimeographed leaflet.

Rimal, Evelyn G. "What Does it Mean to be Educated?" Delta Kappa Gamma Bulletin, 33 (Spring, 1967), 29.

Rollman, Crhis. "Santa Fe: City of Holy Faith," Catholic Digest (September, 1960), 26-32.

Rowan, Bob, et al. "The Teaching of Bilingual Children," Education, 70 (March, 1950), 423-426.

Sanchez, George I. "The Crux of the Dual Language Handicap," 33, New Mexico Review (March, 1954), 13-15, 38.

Santistevan, Henry (ed.). "Viva La Causa! The Rising Expectations of the Mexican-American," IUD Agenda, 2 (July, 1966), 1-28.

Schick, George B. (ed.) Journal of Reading, 10, Published by the International Reading Association (February, 1967), 305-327, -- 40 Doctoral Dissertations reviewed in this issue---Part III.

Schrag, Peter. "Kids, Computers, and Corporations," Saturday Review, Education Editor, James Cass (May 20, 1967), 78-80, 93-96.

Seegers, Scott and Kathleen. "Columbia's Extraordinary Teacher-Builder," Condensed from Latin American Report, Readers Digest, 82 (March, 1965), 111.

Shannon, Lyle W. "Underdeveloped Areas and Their Influence on Personal Development," Journal of Negro Education, 30 (Fall, 1961), 394-395.

Shannon, Pete. "Scholarships Sought by Educational Foundation," Colorado School Journal, 70 (January, 1955), 20.

Shotwell, Louisa R. "What Kind of Harvest?" Presbyterian Life, 14 (July, 1961), 32.

Smith, Herbert F.A. "Foreign Language in the Elementary School?" Journal of the National Education Association, 44 (May, 1955), 271.

Smith, Pamela. "Is Literature Dehumanizing Us?" Christian Science Monitor, Second Section (Saturday, August 5, 1967), 11.

Soleta, Justin. "The Amish," Ave Maria, 103 (January, 1966), 5-10.

Stein, Jay W. "A Wider World of Language for America," Journal of General Education, 14 (January, 1963), 257.

Steinbeck, John. "America and the Americans," Saturday Evening Post, 239th Year Issue (July 2, 1966), 33-47.

Stendler, Celia. "The Montesorri Method," Education Forum, 29 (May, 1965), 431-435.

Stringfellow, William. "The Great Society as a Myth," Catholic World, 205 (May, 1967), 83-89.

Sullivan, Edward J. "Haves and Have-Nots and James Norris," Condensed from The Sign, Catholic Digest, 31 (January, 1967), 83-84.

Sutton, Elizabeth. "Welcome to Our School Jim," Journal of the National Education Association, 46 (January, 1957), 30-32.

_____. "When the Migrant Child Comes to School," Journal of the National Education Association, 50(October, 1961), 32-34.

Taylor, Katherine Whiteside. "A Community-Wide Program of Parent Education," Children, 9 (1962), 9-12.

Thielke, Rosemary. "At Home with Montessori," Ave Maria, 97 (February 9, 1963), 5-8.

Tireman, Lloyd S. "Factors Influencing Learning a Second Language," Education, 81 (January, 1961), 310-313.

Ulich, Robert. "Foreword," Education for an Emerging Age: Newer and Stronger Means, Brameld, T., Harper and Row, Publishers (1965), 2 pages.

Urquides, Maria. "Aqui Se Habla Espanol and English: Tucson's Tale of Two Cultures," Journal of National Education Association, 56 (February, 1967), 1-20.

Van Doren, Mark. "Seekers After Truth," in D. Louis Sharpe (ed.), Why Teach? New York: Henry Holt and Company, 1957.

Verbillion, June. "Linguistics, The Key to Language Instruction?" Education Digest, 28 (May, 1963), 42.

_____. "Bilingual Children," and "Law Degree Scholarships for Spanish-Americans," The Valley Courier (AP), Alamosa, Colorado (April 26, 1967), 1-2.

Wainwright, London. "The Strange New Love Land of the Hippies," Life (March 31, 1967), Section--The View From Here.

Wallace, Almina. "Bilingualism and Retardation," Elementary English, 33 (1956), 303-304.

Washington, Bennetta B. "Books to Make Them Read," Journal of National Education Association, 55 (May, 1966), 20.

White, Eva. "The Inter-Racial School--A Challenge," Delta Kappa Gamma Bulletin, 21 (Spring, 1955), 34-42.

Wilkerson, D.A. "Bibliography on the Education of Socially Disadvantaged Children and Youth," Journal of Negro Education (Summer, 1964), 358-366.

Ziegler, Rosario B. "Spanish in the Elementary Schools," Hispania, 46 (March, 1963), 144.

D. REPORTS

Denver Public Schools. Report-Educational Opportunities for Potential Dropout and for Out-of-School Unemployed Youth. Denver: Denver Public Schools, November 30, 1963.

Denver Public Schools. Tentative Outline of Basic Education and Acculturation. Prepared through the Emily Griffith Opportunity School, Adult, Vocational and Technical Education for Job Opportunity Center, Inc., Denver: Denver Public Schools, 1965.

Fresno County Project. "The Educational Program for Migrant Children," in Teaching Children Who Move With the Crops. Fresno, California: Walter G. Martin, County Superintendent of Schools, September, 1955. 132.

Hansford, Byron W. (Commissioner). Guide to Organization and Administration of Migrant Education Programs: An Aid for Implementation of Educational Opportunities for Children of Migratory Agricultural People. Denver: Colorado State Department of Education, 1963.

Hayman, John L. and J.T. Johnson, Jr. (Project Directors) Title VII Research Project Four Years of Research on the Context of Instructional Television. Denver: Denver Public Schools, 1961.

Hendrix, H.E. (State Superintendent). Course of Study for Elementary Schools of Arizona. Bulletin Number Thirteen. "Instruction of Bilingual Children," Sacramento: California State Printing Office, 1932.

Hodges, Luther H. (Secretary). "White Persons of Spanish Surname," Census: For Release June 3, 1962, United States Department of Commerce, 11 single pages.

Keesee, Elizabeth. Modern Languages in the Elementary School: Teaching Techniques. United States Office of Education, Washington 25, D.C.: Department of Health, Education and Welfare.

Kessee, Elizabeth. References on Foreign Languages in the Elementary
    School. Circular No. 495, Revised, under Title III, National
    Defense Education Act of 1958. Washington 25, D.C.: United
    States Office of Education, Department of Health, Education, and
    Welfare, 1958.

Lanser, Roland L. (Director). Education and Disadvantaged Urban Spanish-
    American Youth. Produced by Teams Attending an NDEA Institute for
    Teachers and Supervisors of Disadvantaged Youth. Sponsored by
    School of Education, University of Denver, Colorado and U.S. Office
    of Education, Washington, D.C.: University of Denver, August, 1966.

Lucey, Robert Emmet, Most Reverend (Sponsor). The Spanish-Speaking of
    the Southwest: A Report of Conferences at Incarnate Word College,
    San Antonio, Texas. Washington 5, D.C.: Social Action Department,
    National Catholic Welfare Conference, 1943.

Morrison, Casey J. (Director). The Puerto Rican Study. "Who Are the
    Puerto Rican Pupils in the New York City Schools?" Sponsored by
    the Board of Education of the City of New York, under a Grant-in-
    Aid from the Fund for Advancement of Education, 1956.

MacGregor, Helen R. and Florence R. Wyckoff. Third Annual Conference
    on Families Who Follow the Crops. Subcommittee on the Migrant
    Child. Report and Recommendations, Visalia, California. Sacramento
    14, California: Governor's Advisory Committee on Children and
    Youth, 1962.

McCanne, Roy. A Study of Approaches to First Grade English Reading
    Instruction for Children from Spanish-Speaking Homes. Cooperative
    Research Project No. 2734, Denver, Colorado: Colorado State
    Department of Education, 1966.

Nance, Afton Dill. Teaching English as a Second Language to Elementary
    School Pupils. Report of Education Study Group, Third Annual
    Conference on Families Who Follow the Crops. Sacramento, California:
    California State Department of Education, 1962.

National Education Association. Education in a Changing Society. Project
    on the Instructional Program of the Public Schools. Prepared by
    Richard I. Miller, Associate Director. Second Printing, Washington,
    D.C. National Education Association, 1964.

Niebuhr, Reinhold. Our Moral and Spiritual Resources for International
    Cooperation. U.S. National Commission for UNESCO, Citizen Con-
    sultation Series. Washington, D.C.: The Commission, 1956.

Parker, W.P. The National Interest and Foreign Languages. Revised
    Edition, U.S. Department of State, National Commission for UNESCO,
    Publication 6389. Washington, D.C.: Government Printing Office,
    January, 1957.

Sargent, John and Pedro T. Orata. Report of the Mission to Thailand. First Edition. Rue Mechain, Paris: Imprimerie Union No. 13, 1950.

Sanchez, George I. Inter-American Education, Occasional Papers IX: Concerning Segregation of Spanish-Speaking Children in the Public Schools. Austin, Texas: The University of Texas, December, 1951.

Sizemore, Mamie. Bibliography for Teachers of English as a Second Language. (Nine pages of very fine references--five bibliographies listed). Phoenix, Arizona: State Department of Public Instruction, Division of Indian Education, 1960.

University of California. Progress Report: Mexican-American Study Projects 1-7. Reports prepared by Division of Research, Graduate School of Business Administration. Los Angeles, California: University of California, 1966.

E. UNPUBLISHED MATERIAL

Bishop. John E., Jr. "A Study of Four Hundred and Three Intellectually Gifted 1957-58 Missouri High School Graduates." Unpublished Doctoral Dissertation, University of Missouri, 1960.

Borrego, Eva R. "Some Educational Aspects Affecting Acculturation of the Spanish-Culture Student in the San Luis Valley." Unpublished Master's Thesis, Adams State College, Alamosa, Colorado, 1946.

Commission on Civil Rights. "Spanish-Speaking People," Staff Paper not for Publication. United States Commission on Civil Rights, 1964.

Condie, LeRoy. "An Experiment in Second Language Instruction of Beginning Indian Children in New Mexico Public Schools." Unpublished Doctoral dissertation, The University of New Mexico, 1961.

Gardner, Donald and Florence Field Gardner. "The Relation of Age-Grade Reading Skills to Environmental-Cultural Factors in the Life-Space of Scholastically Retarded Ethnic Groups in Selected San Luis Valley Public Schools." Unpublished Master's thesis, Adams State College, Alamosa, Colorado, 1965.

Gosen, Sister Mary De Sales. "A Philosophical Study of the Status of Education as a Science," Unpublished Doctoral Dissertation. Catholic University of America, 1960.

Jiron, Mary Jane. "Procedures for Teaching English to Bilingual Children as a Basis for Reading Practices." Unpublished Master's thesis, Adams State College, Alamosa, Colorado, 1956.

Ramirez. "'Wetback' Children in South Texas." Unpublished Master's thesis, Austin, Texas, The University of Texas, 1951.

133

Sandoval, Orlando. L. "Recreational Activities of the Early Spanish
    Settlers in the San Luis Valley," Unpublished Master's thesis,
    Adams State College, Alamosa, Colorado, 1959.

Willeke, Marjorie Joan. "Follow-up Study of Graduates in the San Luis
    Valley," Unpublished Master's thesis, Adams State College, Alamosa,
    Colorado, 1964.

F. OTHER SOURCES

Weber, Dr. Joseph, Superintendent of Schools, Alamosa Re-11J, Personal
    Interview, April 26, 1967.

Lincoln, Sam, Counselor, Alamosa High School, Alamosa, Colorado. Personal
    Interview April 25, 1967.

Ortega, Isaac, Principal East Alamosa and Boyd Schools, Alamosa, Colorado.
    Telephone interview April 24, 1967.

Stephens, Gary, Principal Central School, Alamosa, Colorado. Telephone
    interview April 25, 1967 (later he sent typed information).

Salazar, Delfino, Prominent pioneer business man of San Luis, Colorado.
    Personal interview at San Luis Institute of Arts and Crafts, San
    Luis, Colorado, March, 1946.

G. TESTS

Buros, Oscar K. (ed.). "Stanford Achievement Test," The Sixth Mental
    Measurements Yearbook. Highland Park, New Jersey: The Gryphon
    Press, 1965.

Gilmore, John V. Gilmore Oral Reading Test. New York: Harcourt,
    Brace and World, 1951.

Goodenough, Florence L. and Dale B. Harris. Goodenough-Harris Drawing
    Test. New York: Harcourt, Brace and World, Inc., 1963.

Harris, Dale B. Goodenough-Harris Drawing Test Manual. New York:
    Harcourt, Brace and World, Inc., 1963.

Hildreth, Gertrude H. (et. al.) Metropolitan Readiness Tests. New
    York: Harcourt, Brace and World, Inc. 1963.

Kelly, Truman L. et al. Stanford Achievement Test, Primary I Battery.
    New York: Harcourt, Brace and World, Inc., 1964.

Manuel, Herschel T. Prueba de Habilidad General. Austin, Texas:
    Buidance Testing Associates, 1962.

Manuel, Herschel T. Test of Reading, Level 1 Form CE. Austin, Texas: Guidance Testing Associates, 1965.

Murphy, Helen A. and Donald D. Durrell. Diagnostic Reading Readiness Test. Revised edition. New York: Harcourt, Brace, and World, Inc., 1964.

Pinter, Rudolf, et. al. Pinter-Cunningham Primary Test. New York: Harcourt, Brace, and World, Inc., 1964.

Manual, Herschel T. Test of Reading, Level 1 Form CE. Austin, Texas: Guidance Testing Associates, 1965.

Murphy, Helen A. and Donald D. Durrell. Diagnostic Reading Readiness Test. Revised edition. New York: Harcourt, Brace, and World, Inc., 1964.

Pinter, Rudolf, et. al. Pinter-Cunningham Primary Test. New York: Harcourt, Brace, and World, Inc., 1964.